The Sha[nghai] Maths Project

For the English National Curriculum

Oscar Sharland   ESKH

Series Editor: Professor Lianghuo Fan
UK Curriculum Consultant: Jo-Anne Lees

Practice Book

7

William Collins' dream of knowledge for all began with the publication of his first book in 1819. A self-educated mill worker, he not only enriched millions of lives, but also founded a flourishing publishing house. Today, staying true to this spirit, Collins books are packed with inspiration, innovation and practical expertise. They place you at the centre of a world of possibility and give you exactly what you need to explore it.

Collins. Freedom to teach.

Published by Collins
An imprint of HarperCollins*Publishers* Ltd.
The News Building
1 London Bridge Street
London SE1 9GF

Browse the complete Collins catalogue at
www.collins.co.uk

© HarperCollins*Publishers* Limited 2017
© Professor Lianghuo Fan 2017
© East China Normal University Press Ltd. 2017

10 9 8 7 6 5 4 3 2 1

ISBN: 978-0-00-814468-5

The Shanghai Maths Project (for the English National Curriculum) is a collaborative effort between HarperCollins, East China Normal University Press Ltd. and Professor Lianghuo Fan and his team. Based on the latest edition of the award-wining series of learning resource books, *One Lesson One Exercise*, by East China Normal University Press Ltd. in Chinese, the series of Practice Books is published by HarperCollins after adaptation following the English National Curriculum.

Practice book Year 7 is translated and developed by Professor Lianghuo Fan with assistance of Ellen Chen, Ming Ni, Huiping Xu, Dr. Jane Hui-Chuan Li and Dr. Lionel Pereira-Mendoza, with Jo-Anne Lees as UK curriculum consultant.

British Library Cataloguing in Publication Data
A Catalogue record for this publication is available from the British Library.

Series Editor: Professor Lianghuo Fan
UK Curriculum Consultant: Jo-Anne Lees
Commissioned by Katie Sergeant
Project Managed by Fiona McGlade and Alexander Rutherford
Design by Kevin Robbins and East China Normal University Press Ltd.
Typesetting by East China Normal University Press Ltd.
Cover illustration by Steve Evans
Production by Rachel Weaver
Printed by Grafica Veneta S. p. A

Contents

Chapter 1   Working with numbers

1.1   Four operations with whole numbers: revision (1)

 Learning objective

Solve problems involving all four operations for any integers

 A. Multiple choice questions

(Select the correct answer from the given choices.)

1 To work out 38×99, the most suitable method for quick calculation is (   ).

A. $38 \times 99 = 38 \times 90 + 38 \times 9$

B. $38 \times 99 = 38 \times 100 - 38 \times 1$

C. $38 \times 99 = 30 \times 99 + 8 \times 99$

D. $38 \times 99 = 40 \times 99 - 2 \times 99$

2 To work out $123 + 456 + 544 + 877$, the most suitable method for quick calculation is (   ).

A. $123 + 456 + 544 + 877 = (123 + 456) + (544 + 877)$

B. $123 + 456 + 544 + 877 = 123 + (456 + 544) + 877$

C. $123 + 456 + 544 + 877 = 123 + (456 + 544 + 877)$

D. $123 + 456 + 544 + 877 = (123 + 877) + (456 + 544)$

3 To work out 444×25, the most suitable method for quick calculation is (   ).

A. $444 \times 25 = 444 \times 5 \times 5$

B. $444 \times 25 = 400 \times 25 + 40 \times 25 + 4 \times 25$

C. $444 \times 25 = 4 \times 25 \times 111$

D. $444 \times 25 = 440 \times 25 + 4 \times 25$

4 To find the product of 196 multiplied by the difference between 104 and 5, the correct number sentence is (   ).

A. $196 \times 104 - 5$ 　　　　　　　 B. $(196 \times 104) - 5$

C. $196 \times (104 - 5)$ 　　　　　　 D. $(196 - 104) \times 5$

B. Fill in the blanks

5 Fill in the blanks with $>$, $<$ or $=$.

(a) $27+83$ ____ $83+72$

(b) 54×104 ____ 104×54

(c) $25 \times 8 + 20 \times 8$ ____ $25 + 20 \times 8$

(d) $(14+7) \times 11$ ____ $14 \times 11 + 7 \times 11$

(e) $25 \times 4 + 125 \times 8$ ____ $25 \times 4 \times 125 \times 8$

(f) $(21-4) \times 33$ ____ $21 \times 33 + 4 \times 33$

6 Calculate smartly and write the answers in the blanks. The first one has been done for you.

(a) $125 \times 88 = \underline{125 \times 80 + 125 \times 8} = \underline{10\,000 + 1000} = \underline{11\,000}$

(b) $444 \times 1001 = $ _____ $=$ _____ $=$ _____

(c) $680 \times 11 - 680 = $ _____ $=$ _____ $=$ _____

(d) $33 \times 66 + 33 \times 33 + 33 = $ _____ $=$ _____ $=$ _____

C. Questions that require solutions

(Show your working.)

7 Work these out step by step. (Calculate smartly when possible.)

(a) $4600 + 800 \div 20 - 30 \times 7$

(b) $250 \times 16 \times 125 \times 2$

(c) $368 \times 38 + 38 \times 137 - 38 \times 5$

(d) $(25 \times 52 + 31) \times (77 - 68)$

(e) $72 + 36 \times 2 + 72 + (99 - 27)$

(f) $[(297 - 97) \times 450 - 3000] \div 145$

8 Work these out smartly.

(a) $9999 + 999 + 99 + 9$

(b) 333×999

(c) $20\,062\,006 \times 2005 - 2006 \times 20\,052\,005$

1.2 Four operations with whole numbers: revision (2)

Learning objective

Solve problems involving all four operations for any integers

A. Multiple choice questions

1 Among the following equations, the correct one is (   ).
   A. $6400 \div 125 \div 8 = 6400 \div (125 \times 8)$ B. $547 - 83 - 17 = 547 - (83 - 17)$
   C. $28 + 42 \div 14 = (28 + 42) \div 14$ D. $512 \times 100 - 68 = 512 \times (100 - 68)$

2 From $31 \div 7 = 4$ r 3, the correct one of the following is (   ).
   A. $310 \div 70 = 4$ r 3 B. $310 \div 70 = 4$ r 30
   C. $310 \div 70 = 40$ r 3 D. $310 \div 70 = 40$ r 30

3 The following equations that correctly represent the law or property of the operations indicated are (   ). (Select all the correct answers.)
   A. associative law of addition: $(a + b) + c = a + (b + c)$
   B. commutative law of multiplication: $a \times b = b \times a$
   C. distributive law of multiplication: $a \times (b + c) = a \times b + a \times c$
   D. property of division: $(a \times c) \div (b \times c) = a \div b$ (c is a non-zero number.)

B. Fill in the blanks

4 Using properties of operations, fill in the blanks. The first one has been done for you.
   (a) $4 \times 178 \times 25 = \underline{4 \times 25 \times 178} = \underline{100 \times 178} = \underline{17\ 800}$
   (b) $213 + 1001 + 999 = \underline{\hspace{3cm}} = \underline{\hspace{3cm}} = \underline{\hspace{2cm}}$
   (c) $125 \times (80 + 8) = \underline{\hspace{3cm}} = \underline{\hspace{3cm}} = \underline{\hspace{2cm}}$
   (d) $6000 \div 125 = \underline{\hspace{3cm}} = \underline{\hspace{3cm}} = \underline{\hspace{2cm}}$

5 Using the property of division, write the answers.
   (a) $260 \div 130 = ($ $)$ (b) $750 \div 50 = ($ $)$
   (c) $7200 \div 600 = ($ $)$ (d) $4900 \div 700 = ($ $)$
   (e) $900 \div 150 = ($ $)$ (f) $10\ 000 \div 100 = ($ $)$

C. Questions that require solutions

6 Calculate smartly.

(a) $25 \times (400 + 40)$ (b) $4000 \div 25$

7 Calculate smartly using two different methods.

(a) 8800×125 (b) $88\,000 \div 125$

8 A train is travelling from City A to City B at a speed of 125 km/h. The distance between the two cities is 8000 km. How many hours will it take the train to travel the whole journey?

9 Adrian is reading a comic book which has 120 pages. He has been reading 16 pages per day for 3 days. How many more pages does he need to read to finish half of the book?

1.3 Working with decimals and fractions: revision (3)

Learning objective

Solve problems involving decimals and fractions

A. Multiple choice questions

1. When 0.07 is added to 0.5, it means (   ).

   A. 7 tenths is added to 5 hundredths

   B. 7 tenths is added to 5 tenths

   C. 7 hundredths is added to 5 hundredths

   D. 7 hundredths is added to 5 tenths

2. If $6.55 > 6.\square 6$, the digit in $\square$ can be any integer of (   ).

   A. 0 to 9   B. 0 to 7   C. 0 to 5   D. 0 to 4

3. The result of $\frac{1}{3} \div 2$ is (   ).

   A. $\frac{2}{3}$ B. $\frac{1}{6}$ C. 6   D. $\frac{3}{2}$

4. 6 tens and 6 hundredths make (   ).

   A. 660   B. 60.600   C. 60.06   D. 60.006

B. Fill in the blanks

5. In 59.05, the '5' in the highest value place means 5 _____. The '5' in the least value place means 5 _____.

6. Put 13.03 cm, 13.33 cm, 13.303 m, 130.03 cm, and 13.3 m in order, starting from the greatest: _____

7. 100 times 0.25 is subtracted by the sum of 7.22 and 3.78. The difference is _____.

8 A number 0.42 greater than 25.14 is subtracted by 14.29. The difference is

_____ .

9 Calculate.

(a) $35.4 + 8.53 =$ _____

(b) $4.03 \times 10 \times 100 =$ _____

(c) $56.7 \div$ _____ $= 0.567$

(d) $\dfrac{3}{10} + 0.7 =$ _____

(e) $10 - 6.5 - 3.5 =$ _____

(f) _____ $\times 0.792 = 792$

(g) $0.82 - \dfrac{31}{100} =$ _____

(h) _____ $- 8.25 = 2.48$

C. Questions that require solutions

10 Use your preferred method to calculate.

(a) $29.95 + 7.35 =$

(b) $54 - 5.45 =$

(c) $56.38 - 24.66 - 6.34 =$

(d) $7.35 + 1.66 + 7.34 + 7.65 =$

11 A supermarket bought in 300 kg of apples. It sold 134.6 kg on the second day. The amount was 33.2 kg more than what was sold on the first day. How many kilograms of apples were sold on the first day? How many kilograms of apples were left unsold at the end of the second day?

12 Mr Lee bought 10 pens for £53.60. What was the price he paid for each pen? If he wants to buy 100 pens, how much does he need to pay?

⓭ Find the perimeter of the figure below.

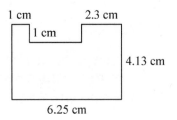

⓮ The table shows the heights of four children in a family（unit: m）.

Name	Jade	Marvin	John	Peg
Height	0.96	1.58	1.61	1.36

（a）What is the average height of the four children?（Correct to 0.01 m.）

（b）Given that the average weight of the children is $38\frac{3}{10}$ kg, what is their total weight?

1.4 Factors, common factors and highest common factors

Learning objective

Use concepts and vocabulary of factors, common factors and highest common factors

A. Multiple choice questions

1. If both 4 and 6 are divisible by a number, then the greatest value of the number is ( ).

   A. 1
   B. 2
   C. 12
   D. 24

2. To write 18 as a product of its prime factors, the correct answer is ( ).

   A. $18 = 2 \times 9$
   B. $18 = 1 \times 18$
   C. $18 = 1 \times 2 \times 9$
   D. $18 = 2 \times 3^2$

3. There are ( ) common factors of 16 and 28.

   A. 1
   B. 2
   C. 3
   D. 4

4. Among the following pairs of numbers, the pair in ( ) do not have common factors except 1.

   A. 13 and 39
   B. 9 and 12
   C. 27 and 28
   D. 26 and 65

5. The incorrect statement of the following is ( ).

   A. Two unequal prime numbers must have no common factors except 1.
   B. Two unequal composite numbers might have no common factors except 1.
   C. A prime number and a composite number might have no common factors.
   D. A prime number and a composite number might have common factors besides 1.

B. Fill in the blanks

6 Write 30 as a product of its prime factors: $30 = $ _____ . Apart from the order of the prime factors, the expression is _____ (fill in 'unique' or 'not unique').

7 The common factor of 8 and 12 is _____ . The common prime factor of 8 and 12 is _____ and the highest common factor is _____ .

8 The highest common factor of 2 and 5 is _____ . The highest common factor of 7 and 13 is _____ .

9 If A and B are positive integers and A is a factor of B, then their highest common factor is _____ . The highest common factor of 7 and 14 is _____ .

10 If $A = 2 \times 2 \times 5$, $B = 2 \times 3 \times 5$, then the highest common factor of A and B is _____ .

11 If the highest common factor of A and B is 15, and $A = 2 \times 3 \times k$, $B = 3 \times k \times 7$, then $k = $ _____ .

C. Questions that require solutions

12 In each of the following pairs of numbers, first write all the factors of each number, and then find the highest common factor. The first one has been done for you.

(a) 12 and 15

(b) 16 and 27

Solution:

The factors of 12 are 1, 2, 3, 4, 6 and 12.

The factors of 15 are 1, 3, 5 and 15.

Therefore, the highest common factor is 3.

(c) 24 and 56

(d) 17 and 119

13 In the following set of numbers, first use a factor tree to obtain the prime factorisation of each number, and then find the highest common factor of these numbers. The first one has been done for you.

(a) 18 and 24

Solution:

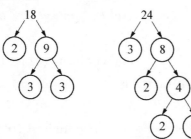

So

$18 = 2 \times 3 \times 3 = 2 \times 3^2$

$24 = 3 \times 2 \times 2 \times 2 = 2^3 \times 3$

Therefore, the highest common factor is $2 \times 3 = 6$.

(b) 36 and 60   (c) 10, 25 and 50   (d) 14, 28 and 56

14 A rectangle is 48 cm long and 30 cm wide. It is cut into several squares that have the same area without any remaining. What is the longest possible side length of a square? How many such squares can the rectangle be cut into?

15 In the figure below, point B is the corner of street ABC. If streetlights are to be installed along one side of the street with equal distance between the lights, and a streetlight must be installed at points A, B and C, at least how many streetlights can be installed along the street?

A ——————————— B

1625 m

1170 m

C

1.5 Multiples, common multiples and lowest common multiples

Learning objective

Use concepts and vocabulary of multiples, common multiples and lowest common multiples

A. Multiple choice questions

1. The lowest common multiple of 4 and 12 is (   ).

   A. 4   B. 12   C. 24   D. 48

2. If a whole number of tiles of 20 cm × 16 cm can be used to exactly cover a square floor, then the side length of the square floor is (   ) of the length and width of the tile.

   A. a common factor   B. the highest common factor

   C. a common multiple   D. the lowest common multiple

3. Among the following statements, the correct one is (   ).

   A. Two different prime numbers do not have the highest common factor.

   B. The product of the highest common factor and the lowest common multiple of two numbers equals the product of the two numbers.

   C. A common factor of two numbers must be less than each of them.

   D. A common multiple of two numbers must be greater than both of them.

B. Fill in the blanks

4. Any two integers have _____ common multiples. Among these common multiples, the least one is called their _____.

5. Within 200, there are _____ common multiples of 12 and 16. The lowest common multiple is _____.

6. If two positive integers, A and B, have no common factors except 1, then their lowest common multiple is _____. The lowest common multiple of 5 and 11 is _____.

7 If A and B are two positive integers and A is a factor of B, then their lowest common multiple is _____ . The lowest common multiple of 3 and 18 is _____ .

8 If $A = 2 \times 2 \times 3$, $B = 2 \times 3 \times 7$, then the lowest common multiple of A and B is _____ . Their lowest common multiple is _____ times the highest common factor.

C. Questions that require solutions

9 In each of the following pairs of numbers, first make a list of multiples of each number, and then find the lowest common multiple. The first one has been done for you.

(a) 6 and 9   (b) 8 and 20

Solution:

The multiples of 6 are 6, 12, 18, 24, 30, 36, ...

The multiples of 9 are 9, 18, 27, 36, 45, 54, ...

Therefore, the lowest common multiple is 36.

(c) 17 and 51   (d) 18 and 42

10 In each of the following groups of numbers, first express each number as the product of its prime factors, and then find their lowest common multiple. The first one has been done for you. (Note: you may use the factor tree to find the prime factorisation of each number.)

(a) 6, 15 and 45   (b) 4, 8 and 16   (c) 15, 18 and 24

Solution:

$6 = 2 \times 3$

$15 = 3 \times 5$

$45 = 3 \times 3 \times 5$

So the lowest common multiple is $2 \times 3 \times 3 \times 5 = 90$.

11 Jane asked her brother Brian about the size of his school choir. Brian said, 'I don't know exactly, but there are 40 to 50 members, and we can line up exactly with 12 people or 8 people in a row.' Jane responded, 'Then I know the answer already.' Do you know what Jane's answer is? Show your working.

12 A team planned to plant trees on one side of a 1.5 km-long road, with equal distance between every tree. They planned to plant a tree every 10 m from one end to the other, so one sign indicator was put in each place. Later, the plan was changed so that a tree would be planted every 12 m. If the signs are still to be used, how many sign indicators can be kept in the same place they were put earlier?

1.6 Multiplying two decimal numbers (1)

Learning objective

Multiply two decimal numbers

A. Multiple choice questions

1. The product of 5.17×3.28 has ( ) decimal place(s).

   A. 1   B. 2   C. 3   D. 4

2. Among the following equations, the correct one is ( ).

   A. $0.83 \times 5.6 = 83 \times 56$ B. $0.83 \times 5.6 = 83 \times 56 \div 10$

   C. $0.83 \times 5.6 = 83 \times 56 \div 100$ D. $0.83 \times 5.6 = 83 \times 56 \div 1000$

3. When one factor is multiplied by 10 and the other factor is multiplied by 100, the product is multiplied by ( ).

   A. 10   B. 100   C. 1000   D. 10 000

B. Fill in the blanks

4. Given $72 \times 25 = 1800$, fill in the blanks.

   (a) $7.2 \times 2.5 =$ _____   (b) $0.72 \times 2.5 =$ _____

   (c) $0.072 \times 0.25 =$ _____   (d) $0.72 \times 0.25 =$ _____

5. Fill in the blanks with suitable numbers to complete the two methods for multiplying 18.6 and 25.4.

   Method 1 (converting to whole numbers):   Method 2 (using the column method):

   18.6×25.4

   $= 186 \times 254 \div$ _____

   $= 47\ 244 \div$ _____

   $=$ _____

```
        1 8. 6  ······ _____ decimal place(s)
    ×   2 5. 4  ······ _____ decimal place(s)
    ─────────────
        7 4 4
      9 3 0
    3 7 2
    ─────────────
    ─────────────  ······ _____ decimal place(s).
```

6 There are _____ decimal places in the product of $0.01 \times 0.02 \times 0.03 \times 0.04 \times \cdots \times 0.09$ in its simplest form.

C. Questions that require solutions

7 Use the column method to calculate.

(a) $8.7 \times 0.9 =$ (b) $0.73 \times 8.5 =$

(c) $20.7 \times 6.9 =$ (d) $8.08 \times 1.05 =$

8 Application problems.

(a) A car travelled from place A to place B at a speed of 78.5 kilometres per hour. It reached place B in 3.8 hours. Find the distance between the two places.

(b) John's family plans to renovate their newly bought house. The lounge has an area of 15.2 m^2 and is to be covered using square tiles of $0.3 \text{ m} \times 0.3 \text{ m}$. Will 180 of the tiles be enough?

(c) On one day in August 2016, the price of unleaded petrol at a petrol station was £1.079 per litre. Jay filled up his car's fuel tank with 50.5 litres of unleaded petrol in the station. How much did he pay?

1.7 Multiplying two decimal numbers (2)

Learning objective

Multiply two decimal numbers

A. Multiple choice questions

① Given $0.58 \times 6.4 = 3.712$, the correct one of the following is (   ).

    A. $580 \times 640 = 37\,120$

    B. $580 \times 640 = 371\,200$

    C. $580 \times 640 = 3\,712\,000$

    D. $580 \times 640 = 37\,120\,000$

② Among the following statements, the correct one is (   ).

    A. The product of two numbers must be greater than each of the two numbers.

    B. The product of two numbers must be less than each of the two numbers.

    C. If the two factors are decimal numbers, the product must be also a decimal number.

    D. If the two factors are decimal numbers, the product is not necessarily a decimal number.

③ The product of 0.024×0.65 has (   ) decimal place(s).

    A. four   B. five

    C. three   D. two

④ The expression that does not have the same answer as $36.5 \times 0.0254 = 0.9271$ is (   ).

    A. 0.365×2.54 B. $254 \times 0.003\,65$

    C. 36.5×2.54 D. 3.65×0.254

⑤ Given that only one of the following is correct, we can estimate that the correct one is (   ).

    A. $0.95 \times 0.35 = 3.325$ B. $4.7 \times 0.82 = 38.54$

    C. $0.78 \times 12.7 = 5.316$ D. $0.46 \times 2.7 = 1.242$

B. Fill in the blanks

6 Put a decimal point in the product of each column multiplication and write the answer below.

(a)
```
        2. 8
 ×      5. 3
        8 4
    1 4 0
    1 4 8 4
```
Answer: _____

(b)
```
        0. 3 5
 ×      4. 6
      2 1 0
    1 4 0
    1 6 1 0
```
Answer: _____

(c)
```
      0. 1 6
 × 0. 2 1
        1 6
      3 2
      3 3 6
```
Answer: _____

7 Based on the first product on the left, write the other products in the columns accordingly.

Factor	4.8	4.8	4.8	4.8	4.8
Factor	15	1.5	1	0.15	0.015
Product	72	_____	_____	_____	_____

8 Fill in the blanks with $>$, $<$ or $=$ without working out the answers.

(a) 2.56×12.8 _____ 2.56 (b) 7.95×0.8 _____ 7.95
(c) 0.78×12.7 _____ 12.7 (d) 1.003×0.9 _____ 0.9

9 Using the result $4.1 \times 3.2 = 13.12$, write the product of each multiplication below.

$4.1 \times 32 =$ _____ $0.41 \times 320 =$ _____ $0.041 \times 32 =$ _____
$41 \times 320 =$ _____ $0.41 \times 3.2 =$ _____ $4.1 \times 0.032 =$ _____

10 Based on the equation $75 \times 26 = 1950$, fill in the blanks with suitable numbers. How many combinations can you write?

$19.5 =$ _____ $\times$ _____ $=$ _____ $\times$ _____ $=$ _____ $\times$ _____
$1.95 =$ _____ $\times$ _____ $=$ _____ $\times$ _____ $=$ _____ $\times$ _____

C. Questions that require solutions

11 Use the column method to calculate.

(a) $1.28 \times 0.35 =$

(b) $5.26 \times 2.04 =$

(c) $3.32 \times 0.045 =$

(d) $3.02 \times 0.016 =$

12 The speed of a bicycle is 9.5 km/h, while the speed of a car is 12.5 times that of the bicycle. How many kilometres does the car travel in 1.5 hours?

1.8 Division by a decimal number (1)

Learning objective

Divide a number by a decimal number

A. Multiple choice questions

1. The correct answer to $0.1 \div 0.5$ is (　　).

    A. 2 　　　　　 B. 0.2 　　　　　 C. 5 　　　　　 D. 0.5

2. Among the following equations, the correct one is (　　).

    A. $5.87 \div 0.025 = 587 \div 25$

    B. $0.9 \div 0.04 = 90 \div 4$

    C. $1.378 \div 1.5 = 137.8 \div 15$

    D. $475 \div 0.29 = 4750 \div 29$

3. Given $32 \div 12.5 = 2.56$, the correct one of the following is (　　).

    A. $32 \div 1.25 = 2.56$ 　　　　　 B. $0.32 \div 0.125 = 0.256$

    C. $32 \div 0.125 = 256$ 　　　　　 D. $0.32 \div 1.25 = 0.0256$

B. Fill in the blanks

4. Among the following, the divisions that have the same answer are (a) and (C), (b) and _____, (c) and _____, (d) and _____ respectively.

    (a)

    $8.9 \overline{)3\ 8\ 2.7}$

    (b)

    $8.9 \overline{)3\ 8\ 2\ 7\ 0}$

    (c)

    $0.89 \overline{)3\ 8\ 2.7}$

    (d)

    $8.9 \overline{)3\ 8.2\ 7}$

    (A)

    $89 \overline{)3\ 8\ 2.7}$

    (B)

    $89 \overline{)3\ 8\ 2\ 7\ 0}$

    (C)

    $89 \overline{)3\ 8\ 2\ 7}$

    (D)

    $89 \overline{)3\ 8\ 2\ 7\ 0\ 0}$

5 Observe carefully and fill in both ( ) and _____ with suitable numbers.

$7 \div 1.4 =$ _____ $6 \div 0.12 =$ _____ $0.091 \div 0.005 =$ _____

$\downarrow \times 10 \ \downarrow \times 10 \quad \uparrow$ $\downarrow \times (\ ) \ \downarrow \times (\ ) \quad \uparrow$ $\downarrow \times (\ ) \ \downarrow \times (\ ) \quad \uparrow$

$70 \div 14 =$ _____   ___ $\div$ ___ $=$ _____   ___ $\div$ ___ $=$ _____

C. Questions that require solutions

6 Use the column method to calculate. The first one has been done for you. (Check answers to the questions marked $*$.)

   (a) $10.8 \div 0.24 = 4.25$ (b) $2.05 \div 20.5 =$ (c) $6 \div 7.5 =$

```
           4. 2 5
    2.4 ) 1 0. 8
         9. 6
    ----------
         1. 2 0
         1. 2 0
    ----------
              0
```

$*$ (d) $4.75 \div 0.38 =$ (e) $0.324 \div 0.18 =$ $*$ (f) $0.08 \div 2.5 =$

7 Application problems.

   (a) Bob wants to cut a wire 40 m long into pieces so that each piece is 2.5 m long. How many pieces will he get?

   (b) A clothing factory made 76 800 sets of clothes in the first half of a year, which was 1.6 times the production of the second half of the year. How many sets of clothes did the factory produce in the year in total?

(c) A car travelled for 2.5 hours from place A to place B, which were 207.9 km apart. The car took 3 hours on the return journey. What was the average speed of the car for the round trip?

(d) A rectangular wall has a length of 8.01 m and a width of 2.5 m. If one litre of paint can paint 4.5 m^2, how many litres of paint is needed to paint both sides of the wall?

1.9   Division by a decimal number (2)

Learning objective

Divide a number by a decimal number

A. Multiple choice questions

1 Without calculation, compare the following divisions. The greatest quotient is obtained in (   ).

A. $0.75 \div 0.13$ B. $0.075 \div 1.3$ C. $7.5 \div 1.3$ D. $75 \div 1.3$

2 Without calculation, the result of comparing the quotients of ① $8.256 \div 2.14$, ② $8256 \div 2.14$, ③ $82.56 \div 0.214$, ④ $0.8256 \div 0.0214$ should be (   ).

A. ② > ③ > ④ > ①   B. ② > ③ > ① > ④

C. ③ > ② > ④ > ①   D. ③ > ② > ① > ④

3 Given $M > 0$, the incorrect one of the following is (   ).

A. $M \div 0.1 > M$ B. $M \times 1.1 > M$

C. $M \div 1.1 > M$ D. $M \times 0.99 < M$

B. Fill in the blanks

4   Observe carefully and complete the table.

Dividend	1.2				
Divisor	0.015	0.15	1	1.5	15
Quotient	_____	_____	_____	_____	_____

5 Without calculation, fill in _____ with $>$, $<$ or $=$.

(a) $12.1 \div 1.1$ _____ 12.1 (b) $10.8 \div 0.9$ _____ 10.8

(c) $3.6 \div 0.9$ _____ 3.6 (d) $1.37 \div 0.991$ _____ 1.37

(e) $8.9 \div 1.25$ _____ 8.9 (f) 3.8×100 _____ $3.8 \div 0.01$

(g) $63.8 \div 0.9$ _____ 63.8×0.9 (h) 78×0.9 _____ 78×1.1

(i) $26.25 \div 1.05$ _____ 26.25×1.05

C. Questions that require solutions

6 Use the column method to calculate. (Check answers to the questions marked * .)

(a) $22.1 \div 0.17 =$　　　　　　　　(b) $0.216 \div 0.72 =$

* (c) $6.24 \div 0.26 =$　　　　　　　* (d) $0.303 \div 0.025 =$

7 Work these out step by step.

(a) $2.4 \div 0.8 \times 0.9$　　　　　　(b) $35.65 \div 4.6 \times 1.3$

(c) $0.58 \times 4.3 \div 0.2$

8 Application problems.

(a) Dan wants to cut a rope of 18.6 m into pieces that are 2.5 m long. How many pieces can he cut the rope into? How many metres will be left over?

(b) A total of 29 litres of drinking water is poured into 1.25-litre bottles. How many bottles can be filled? How many litres of the drinking water will be left over?

(c) A car park charges a minimum of £5 for each entry for up to two hours and £2.50 for every extra hour. One day, Mr Wilton parked his car there. He paid £20 when he left the car park. For how many hours at most did he park his car?

1.10 Division of fractions (1)

Learning objective

Divide an integer or a fraction by a fraction and use the notation of reciprocals

A. Multiple choice questions

1 Among the following statements, the correct one is (   ).

A. The product of a number and its reciprocal is always 1.

B. The sum of a number and its reciprocal is zero.

C. The reciprocal of a number must be less than the number itself.

D. Any number has a reciprocal.

2 Among the following statements, the correct one is (   ).

A. The expression $12 + \frac{3}{4}$ is to find the sum of 12 lots of $\frac{3}{4}$.

B. The expression $\frac{5}{9} \div \frac{1}{12}$ is to find $\frac{1}{12}$ of $\frac{5}{9}$.

C. The sum of $\frac{3}{4}$ and its reciprocal is $2\frac{1}{12}$.

D. The expression $\frac{4}{5} \div 5$ is to find 5 times $\frac{4}{5}$.

B. Fill in the blanks

3 If $a \neq 0$, the reciprocal of a is _____. If $p \neq 0$ and $q \neq 0$, the reciprocal of $\frac{p}{q}$ is _____.

4 The reciprocal of $\frac{1}{4}$ is _____. The reciprocal of 10 is _____.

5 The reciprocal of _____ is $\frac{1}{12}$. The reciprocal of _____ is $1\frac{1}{3}$.

6 The reciprocal of 1 is _____.

7 The reciprocal of 7.5 is _____ .

8 The reciprocal of the product of $\frac{1}{4}$ and $\frac{2}{3}$ is _____ .

C. Questions that require solutions

9 Calculate the following. The first one has been done for you.

(a) $1 \div \frac{4}{7}$

(b) $1 \div \frac{3}{5}$

Solution: $1 \div \frac{4}{7} = 1 \times \frac{7}{4}$

$\qquad = \frac{7}{4}$

(c) $1 \div 1\frac{3}{5}$

(d) $1 \div 2\frac{1}{3}$

(e) $1\frac{3}{5} \div 4\frac{1}{6}$

(f) $8\frac{4}{5} \div 4\frac{2}{5} - \frac{3}{4} \div 2\frac{1}{8}$

10 Given that the reciprocal of a is 4 and the reciprocal of b is $1\frac{1}{3}$, find the value of a times b .

11 The product of a fraction multiplied consecutively by $\frac{3}{5}$, $2\frac{2}{3}$ and $1\frac{1}{4}$ is the least positive integer. Find this fraction.

1.11 Division of fractions (2)

Learning objective

Divide an integer or a fraction by a fraction and use the notation of reciprocals

A. Multiple choice questions

1 The correct calculation of the following is (　　).

A. $\dfrac{\frac{3}{12}}{7} = \dfrac{3}{12} \div 7 = \dfrac{1}{28}$

B. $3 \div \dfrac{4}{5} \div \dfrac{4}{5} = 3 \div \left(\dfrac{4}{5} \div \dfrac{4}{5}\right) = 3$

C. $\dfrac{3 + \frac{1}{4}}{6} = 3 + \dfrac{1}{4} \div 6 = 3\dfrac{1}{24}$

D. $\dfrac{21}{23} \times \dfrac{76}{23} \div \dfrac{38}{23} = \dfrac{21}{23} \times \left(\dfrac{76}{23} \div \dfrac{38}{23}\right) = \dfrac{42}{23}$

2 In a Christmas sale，the promotional price of a large screen TV was £6480 after a discount of $\dfrac{1}{10}$. The original price of the TV was (　　).

A. £7128 　　　　B. £5832 　　　　C. £7200 　　　　D. £7920

B. Fill in the blanks

3 The reciprocal of $1\dfrac{3}{4}$ is _____.

4 The reciprocal of _____ is $\dfrac{2}{5}$.

5 _____ of $\dfrac{1}{8}$ is 5.

6 $2\dfrac{1}{2}$ times _____ is $1\dfrac{1}{2}$.

7 _____ $\times \dfrac{4}{7} = 1\dfrac{2}{5}$.

8 $\dfrac{5}{8} \div$ _____ $= \dfrac{1}{8}$.

C. Questions that require solutions

9 Calculate.

(a) $3\dfrac{1}{3} \div \dfrac{9}{2}$

(b) $1\dfrac{1}{3} \div 5\dfrac{3}{5}$

(c) $1\dfrac{7}{8} \div 1\dfrac{1}{14} \div 14$

(d) $1\dfrac{1}{14} \div \left(14 \div 1\dfrac{5}{9}\right)$

10 A cheetah can run $1\dfrac{2}{3}$ km per minute. In how many minutes can it run $4\dfrac{1}{2}$ km?

11 When solving a problem involving operations of fractions, Tad mistakenly took the multiplication of $2\dfrac{2}{5}$ as division of $2\dfrac{2}{5}$, and got the answer $\dfrac{125}{288}$. What is the correct answer to the question?

12 Complete the flow chart of calculation. Write a suitable number in each box.

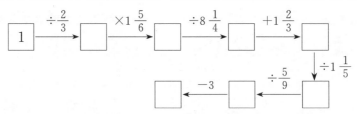

1.12 Converting between fractions and decimals

 Learning objective

Convert fractions to and from terminating and recurring decimals

 A. Multiple choice questions

1 Among the fractions $\frac{1}{8}$, $\frac{3}{12}$, $\frac{2}{11}$, $\frac{3}{9}$ and $\frac{5}{16}$, (   ) of them can be converted to terminating decimals.

    A. 2   B. 3

    C. 4   D. 5

2 Among the following fractions, the greatest one is (   ).

    A. $\frac{17}{30}$ B. $\frac{13}{32}$

    C. $\frac{15}{35}$ D. $\frac{11}{36}$

3 7.777 is a (   ).

    A. recurring decimal   B. non-terminating decimal

    C. terminating decimal   D. none of the above

 B. Fill in the blanks

4 In recurring decimal $0.125\,125\ldots$, the recurring part is _____. It can be denoted as _____.

5 The recurring part of the recurring decimal $1.234\,564\,56\ldots$ is _____. It can be denoted as _____. If it is kept to 4 decimal places, it can be written as _____.

6 42 minutes = _____ hour (in fraction) = _____ hour (in decimal).

7 1428 g = _____ kg (in fraction) = _____ kg (in decimal).

8 Convert the following fractions or mixed numbers to recurring decimals.

(a) $\dfrac{2}{9} = $ _____

(b) $1\dfrac{3}{11} = $ _____

(c) $\dfrac{32}{15} = $ _____

(d) $\dfrac{23}{6} = $ _____

C. Questions that require solutions

9 The lengths of two pieces of wood are $51\dfrac{3}{4}$ cm and 29.6 cm, respectively. If they are joined together and the overlapping part is 5.4 cm long, what is the length of the two pieces of wood after they are joined?

10 Convert the following fractions to recurring decimals.

(a) $\dfrac{1}{3}$

(b) $\dfrac{3}{11}$

(c) $\dfrac{1}{24}$

(d) $\dfrac{7}{15}$

11 Put the following numbers in order, starting from the least.

(a) $\dfrac{5}{8}$, $0.6\dot{2}$, $\dfrac{2}{5}$, $0.\dot{4}\dot{0}$

(b) $4\dfrac{19}{20}$, $4.\dot{9}\dot{5}$, $4.9\dot{5}$, $4\dfrac{24}{25}$, $4.\dot{9}0\dot{5}$

12 Convert the following fractions to decimals.

$\dfrac{1}{9} =$ _____ $\dfrac{2}{9} =$ _____

$\dfrac{3}{9} =$ _____ $\dfrac{4}{9} =$ _____

$\dfrac{5}{9} =$ _____ $\dfrac{6}{9} =$ _____

$\dfrac{7}{9} =$ _____ $\dfrac{14}{9} =$ _____

$\dfrac{17}{9} =$ _____

Observe the above and look for patterns. Can you now convert the following fractions to decimals quickly?

$\dfrac{25}{9} =$ _____ $\dfrac{30}{9} =$ _____

$\dfrac{52}{9} =$ _____ $\dfrac{73}{9} =$ _____

1.13 Calculating interest and percentage[1]

Learning objective

Solve problems involving percentage and simple interest in financial mathematics

A. Multiple choice questions

1. Mr Ling made a fixed deposit of £1000 for a period of one year, and the deposit account bears an interest rate of 0.25% each month. In this case, £1000 is called ( ), the monthly interest rate is ( ), the annual interest rate is ( ) and without paying tax, the accrued amount at the end is ( ).

   A. £1030

   B. 3%

   C. 0.25%

   D. principal amount

2. Among the following calculations involving interest, the incorrect one is ( ).

   A. Interest = principal amount × interest rate × time

   B. Annual interest rate = 12 × monthly interest rate

   C. Accrued amount = principal amount + interest

   D. Interest after tax = accrued amount × tax rate − principal amount

3. A man borrows £50 000 from a bank without repayment for a period of 3 years. The monthly interest rate is 0.7%. The accrued amount that he needs to pay back to the bank at the end of the three years is ( ) pounds.

   A. $5 \times 0.7\% \times 3$

   B. $50\,000 \times 0.7\% \times 36$

   C. $50\,000(1 + 0.7\% \times 36)$

   D. $5 + 5 \times 0.7\% \times 12 \times 3$

---

[1] Unless otherwise stated, we use the term 'interest' in this book to refer to 'simple interest', that is, the interest is only paid on the principal amount, but not on the interest accumulated over previous periods.

B. Fill in the blanks

4 Given that the taxable amount is £150 000 and the tax rate is 10.5%, the amount of tax to pay is £_____ .

5 Given that the taxable amount is £40 000 and the amount of tax paid is £3604, the tax rate is _____ .

6 A company paid £693 000 for tax at a tax rate of 23% on the profit it made in a year. The company made a profit of £_____ in the year.

7 If the annual interest rate is 5% for a fixed deposit of £80 000 over a period of 3 years, then the accrued amount after 3 years is £_____ .

8 Alvin's family deposited £50 000 in a bank and had the accrued amount of £52 430 after a period. If the annual interest rate is 2.43%, then his family has deposited the money for a period of _____ years.

C. Questions that require solutions

9 Lily deposited £20 000 in a bank for a period of one year. The annual interest rate was 2.25% and the tax rate was 20% on the interest earned. How much is the accrued amount of money Lily received after tax at the end of one year?

10 A financial institution has released a new financial policy. The table summarises the adjustment of interest rates offered for fixed deposit accounts over different periods of time.

Interest rates (before and after change)

Duration of deposit	Annual interest rate	
	Before	**After**
1 year	3.60%	2.52%
2 years	4.14%	3.06%
3 years	4.77%	3.60%
5 years	5.13%	3.87%

(a) For a three-year fixed deposit of £10 000, the interest earned under the new interest rate will be £(   ) less than the interest that would be earned under the original interest rate.

(b) Lee's family would like to deposit £50 000 for a period of two years. Lee suggests opening a two-year fixed deposit account for the money. His brother suggests opening a one-year fixed deposit first and at the end of one year, withdrawing the accrued amount and then re-depositing the total amount for a second year. Whose suggestion will earn more interest? By how much is it more? (Round your answer to integers.)

Unit test 1

A. Multiple choice questions

1 Among the following equations, the incorrect one is (   ).

A. $8400 \div 300 = 28$ B. $45 - 45 \div 9 = 0$

C. $800 \div 2 \times 7 = 2800$ D. $240 \times 0.5 - 40 = 80$

2 Among the following equations, the incorrect one is (   ).

A. $225 - 34 - 66 = 225 - (34 + 66)$

B. $8.3 \times 6.2 + 0.83 \times 38 = 0.83 \times (6.2 + 3.8)$

C. $369 \div (3 \times 3) = 369 \div 3 \div 3$

D. $44 \div 0.4 = 440 \div 40$

3 The highest common factor of 12 and 20 is (   ).

A. 1   B. 2   C. 4   D. 8

4 The lowest common multiple of 6 and 9 is (   ).

A. 1   B. 6   C. 18   D. 54

5 Among the following, the expression that has the same product as 10.6×1.74 is (   ).

A. 1.06×1.74 B. 1.06×174

C. 0.106×1740 D. 1060×0.0174

6 Among the following equations, the value of a in (   ) is less than 1.

A. $6.3 \div a = 1$ B. $a \times 0.3 = 1$

C. $a \div 0.1 = 1$ D. $0.8 \times a = 1$

7 If £5000 is deposited in a savings account at an annual interest rate of 3.6% for three years, the accrued amount before tax at the end of three years is (   ).

A. $5000 \times (1 + 3 \times 3.6\%)$ B. $5000 + 5000 \times 3.6\%$

C. $5000 \times 3 \times 3.6\%$ D. $5000 \times 3 \times (1 + 3.6\%)$

B. Fill in the blanks

8 Work these out mentally. Write the answers.

(a) $0.3 \div 0.01 = $ _____

(b) $1.2 \times 0.4 = $ _____

(c) $0.9 \div 4.5 \times 0.2 = $ _____

(d) $0.125 \times 0.7 \times 0.8 = $ _____

9 The reciprocal of $8\frac{1}{4}$ is _____. The reciprocal of 1.8 is _____.

10 The recurring decimal $0.323\,232\ldots$ can be denoted as _____.

11 The recurring part of the recurring decimal $0.103\,103\,103\ldots$ is _____.

12 The reciprocal of the product of $\frac{1}{4}$ and $\frac{2}{3}$ is _____.

13 In $\frac{7}{16}$, $\frac{3}{25}$ and $\frac{5}{12}$, the fraction that cannot be converted to a terminating decimal is _____.

14 Converting the fraction $\frac{17}{22}$ to a recurring decimal, the result is _____.

15 If the monthly interest rate of a savings account is 0.12%, the annual interest rate is _____.

16 If $A = 2 \times 3$, $B = 3 \times 5$, then the lowest common multiple of A and B is _____.

17 If the sum of two consecutive even numbers is 18, then the lowest common multiple of these two numbers is _____.

18 In 3, 5, 12 and 20, there are _____ pairs of numbers that have no common factors except 1.

C. Questions that require solutions

⑲ Work these out step by step. (Calculate smartly when possible.)

(a) $117 - 56 - 44 + 83$

(b) $680 \times 89 \div 34$

(c) $2200 \div 125$

(d) $(137 \times 31 - 31 \times 12) \times 8$

⑳ In each of the following groups of numbers, find the highest common factor and the lowest common multiple. (Show the factor tree for each number.)

(a) 18 and 54

(b) 21 and 35

(c) 24 and 42

(d) 10, 12 and 18

㉑ Use the column method to calculate. (Check the answer to the question marked ∗ .)

(a) 12.5×0.82

(b) 0.47×0.28

(Round to the nearest tenth)

(c) $4.8 \div 0.43$ * (d) $1.296 \div 0.18$

   (Round to the nearest hundredth)

22 Calculate.

(a) $13.2 \div 1\frac{1}{5} \times \frac{15}{22}$ (b) $18\frac{1}{3} \div 1\frac{5}{6} \times \frac{9}{22} \div 1\frac{1}{14}$

(c) $2\frac{1}{5} \times \frac{7}{11} - 1\frac{5}{6} \div 7\frac{1}{3}$ (d) $4\frac{1}{2} + 4.5 \times 2\frac{7}{8} + \frac{1}{8} \div \frac{2}{9}$

(e) $5.4 \times 6.8 + 5.4 \times 4.2 - 5.4$ (f) $8.58 - 8.58 \div 3.3 \times 2.5$

23 A bottle can be filled with 0.55 litres of water. How many bottles will 100 litres of water fill? How many litres will be left over?

24 The weight of a chicken egg is 0.061 kg. The weight of an ostrich egg is 1.55 kg. How many times heavier is an ostrich egg than a chicken egg?

25 The area of a rectangle is 28 cm^2. Both the length a and the width b are whole numbers and their lowest common multiple is 14. What is the perimeter of the rectangle?

26 A company received a loan of £80 000 from a bank with an annual interest rate of 6.9% for a period of 5 years. How much accrued amount does the company need to pay back to the bank at the end of 5 years?

27 Mr Johnson made a fixed deposit of £5000 in a bank at the annual interest rate of 2.7% for two years. He will have to pay tax on the interest at the rate of 5% when he withdraws the money. At the end of two years, how much will he need to pay for the interest tax? How much money will he receive?

Chapter 2   Rational numbers

2.1   The meaning of rational numbers

 Learning objective

Understand the meaning of rational numbers and compare them

A. Multiple choice questions

1 In the following four places, the lowest one is (   ).
   A. 80 metres above sea level   B. -20 metres above sea level
   C. -80 metres above sea level   D. 20 metres below sea level

2 In the numbers 15, -7.35, 0, $\dfrac{4}{5}$, $0.\overset{\cdot}{3}0\overset{\cdot}{3}$, $\dfrac{11}{7}$ and $0.101\,001\,000\,1\ldots$, there are
   (   ) rational numbers.
   A. 4   B. 5   C. 6   D. 7

3 Among the following statements, the incorrect one is (   ).
   A. Rational numbers can be classified into two groups: positive numbers and
       negative numbers.
   B. Rational numbers can be classified into two groups: integers and fractions.
   C. All terminating decimals and recurring decimals are rational numbers.
   D. A rational number is any number that can be written as a ratio of two integers.

B. Fill in the blanks

4 If a rotation of $100°$ anticlockwise is recorded as $-100°$, then a rotation of $90°$
   clockwise can be recorded as _____ .

5 The least non-negative number is _____ ; the greatest negative integer is
   _____ .

6 Negative integers that are not less than -3 are _____ .

⑦ Write two numbers satisfying the conditions: positive numbers but not integers. The numbers are _____ .

⑧ According to available data, the highest temperature recorded in the London area was 38.1℃ in August, 2003 and the lowest temperature was −16.1℃ in January, 1962. The difference between the two extremes is _____ ℃ .

⑨ Rewrite the following statements using positive integers. The first one has been done for you.

Using negative numbers	**Using positive numbers**
Walk −20 metres west.	<u>Walk 20 metres east.</u>
Make a profit of − £78.	_____
The temperature rose by −8℃.	_____
The cost of a product reduced by −20%.	_____

C. Questions that require solutions

⑩ Fill in the circles with suitable numbers given below.

$$12 \quad −1 \quad 0.25 \quad 0 \quad \frac{1}{4} \quad 80\% \quad −0.4$$

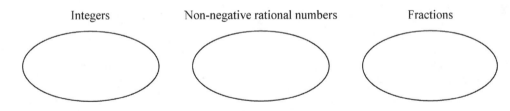

Integers   Non-negative rational numbers   Fractions

⑪ If a is an integer and $−2 \leqslant a < \dfrac{11}{3}$, find all the possible values of a.

12 The normal water level of a river is 22 m. A hydrometric station measured the water levels for 7 consecutive days and recorded the differences from the normal level as follows:

$+1.5$ m, -1.0 m, 0 m, -0.8 m, $+2.2$ m, $+1.8$ m, $+1.2$ m.

What was the average water level of the river on these 7 days?

13 In the diagram below, the numbers in the two ovals represent the sets of integers and non-negative numbers, respectively.

(a) Write three rational numbers in each of part A, part B and part C.

(b) Can you tell what types of numbers A, B and C represent, respectively?

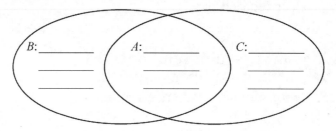

Integers   Non-negative numbers

2.2　Number lines

Learning objective

Understand and use number lines to represent numbers and solve related problems

A. Multiple choice questions

1 For any number a, $-a$ must be (　　).

A.　a positive number
B.　a negative number
C.　a non-negative number
D.　none of the above are correct

2 On a number line, if a and b are on the different sides of origin O but have the same distance from O, and $a \neq 0$, $b \neq 0$, then (　　) is not necessarily true.

A. $a + b = 0$
B. $a - b > 0$
C. $a \times b < 0$
D. $\dfrac{a}{b} = -1$

3 If $0 < a < 1$, then the relationship among a, $-a$ and $\dfrac{1}{a}$ is (　　).

A. $-a > a > \dfrac{1}{a}$
B. $a > \dfrac{1}{a} > -a$
C. $\dfrac{1}{a} > -a > a$
D. $\dfrac{1}{a} > a > -a$

B. Fill in the blanks

4 A number line is a straight line that has its ＿＿＿＿＿＿＿, ＿＿＿＿＿＿＿ and ＿＿＿＿＿＿＿.

5 If $a = -a$, then a is ＿＿＿＿＿.

6 If a number has the same distance from origin O as $a - b$ but lies on the different side of origin O, then the number is ＿＿＿＿＿.

7 If $-a$ is 0.2, then the reciprocal of a is ＿＿＿＿＿.

8 There are ＿＿＿＿＿ integers whose distances to the origin are less than $\dfrac{9}{4}$.

9 Given that point A represents $\dfrac{3}{4}$ on the number line and point B represents -1, then point A is on the _____ side of point B and the distance from point A to point B is _____ units.

C. Questions that require solutions

10 What numbers are represented by points A, B and C on the number line below?

A : _____ B : _____ C : _____

11 Show the points on the number line.

point A : The least positive integer

point B : The number which adds to $\dfrac{9}{4}$ is 0

point C : The number whose reciprocal is -0.6

point D : The point that will coincide with point B after moving 3 units to the left

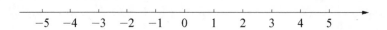

12 Given that the sum of $3x$ and $2(x-1)$ is 0, find the value of x.

13 Given that point A represents -2 on a number line, point A coincides with point B after moving 4 units to the right on the number line, and the distance from point C to point A is 3 times the distance from point C to point B, find the number that point C represents.

14 The numbers points A, B and C represent on the number line are 0, -1 and x, respectively. The distance between point C and point A is greater than the distance between point C and point B. Find the range of the value of x.

2.3 Addition of rational numbers (1)

Learning objective

Add rational numbers including both positive and negative numbers

A. Multiple choice questions

1. If the sum of two numbers is negative, then these two numbers (   ).
   A. must be both positive numbers
   B. must be both negative numbers
   C. must have opposite signs (i.e., one is positive and the other is negative)
   D. must contain at least one negative number

2. If $a + b = 0$, then the correct statement of the following is (   ).
   A. a and b are reciprocals to each other
   B. a and b are equal
   C. both a and b are 0
   D. a and $-b$ are equal

3. The following statement that is incorrect is (   ).
   A. The sum of a negative rational number a and a negative number is always less than a.
   B. The sum of a negative rational number a and a positive number is always greater than a.
   C. The sum of a negative rational number a and a positive number may be negative.
   D. The sum of a negative rational number a and a negative number may be positive.

B. Fill in the blanks

4 If $a > 0$, $b > 0$, then the sign of their sum is _____.

If $a < 0$, $b < 0$, then the sign of their sum is _____.

If $a > 0$, $b < 0$, then:

(i) the sign of their sum is _____ when $a > -b$ (for example, $2 + (-1.5)$ is

_____)

(ii) the sign of their sum is _____ when $a < -b$ (for example, $2 + (-2.5)$ is

_____).

If $a < 0$, $b > 0$, then:

(iii) the sign of their sum is _____ when $b > -a$ (for example, $-3 + 4$ is

_____)

(iv) the sign of their sum is _____ when $b < -a$ (for example, $-3 + 2$ is

_____).

5 $5 + ($ $) = -3$, $-3 + ($ $) = -5$.

6 Calculate: $\left(-1\frac{1}{2}\right) + \left(-2\frac{1}{3}\right) = $ _____.

7 Calculate: $\left(-1\frac{1}{2}\right) + 2\frac{1}{3} = $ _____.

8 Calculate: $1\frac{1}{2} + \left(-2\frac{1}{3}\right) = $ _____.

9 Without calculation, write the sign of the sum in each blank.

(a) $(-5) + \left(-7\frac{5}{21}\right)$: _____   (b) $(-0.01) + 0$: _____

(c) $\left(+8\frac{1}{9}\right) + \left(-9\frac{1}{8}\right)$: _____   (d) $7 + (-6)$: _____

10 The opening price of a stock was £12.50. It rose by 4% in the morning and £0.40 in the afternoon. The closing price of the stock for the day was £_____.

C. Questions that require solutions

11 The difference of a number and $-\frac{1}{2}$ is equal to the sum of $-\frac{1}{5}$ and $-2\frac{3}{10}$. Find the number.

12 A road maintenance team inspected a road from a road station along the east-west direction. Assuming that the eastbound direction is positive and the westbound direction is negative, the team's travel records of the day were as follows (unit: km):

1st time	2nd time	3rd time	4th time	5th time	6th time	7th time
-4	$+7$	-9	$+8$	$+6$	-5	-2

(a) How far was the team away from the road station when their work was completed on the day? In which direction of the road station was the team?

(b) At the _____ time, the team was the farthest away from the road station.

(c) If the fuel consumption was 0.2 litres per km, what was the total amount of fuel consumption on the day?

13 Find the pattern and fill in the numbers. Then answer the questions.
$-1.2, -1, -0.8, -0.6, $ _____ , ...

(a) What is the 16th number?

(b) What is the sum of the first 16 numbers?

2.4　Addition of rational numbers (2)

Learning objective

Add rational numbers including both positive and negative numbers

A.　Multiple choice questions

1. The result of $(+6)+(-3)+(+7)+(-5)$ is (　　).

   A. -7 　　　　B. -5 　　　　C. 5 　　　　D. -3

2. Based on the diagram below, the following conclusion that is incorrect is (　　).

   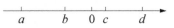

   A. $a+b<0$ 　　B. $c+d>0$ 　　C. $b+c>0$ 　　D. $c+a<0$

3. The sum of all integers that are greater than -3 but less than 5 is (　　).

   A. 7 　　　　B. -7 　　　　C. 0 　　　　D. 5

B.　Fill in the blanks

4. Calculate: $(+16)+(-12)+(-4)=$ _____.

5. Calculate: $\left(-8\frac{2}{3}\right)+\left(-3\frac{1}{5}\right)+6\frac{2}{3}=$ _____.

6. Calculate: $4.7+(-6)+(-7.5)=$ _____.

7. Calculate: $3.25+(-100)+\left(-3\frac{3}{4}\right)=$ _____.

8. Calculate: $1\frac{3}{4}+\left(-1\frac{1}{2}\right)+\left(-\frac{5}{6}\right)+0.25=$ _____.

C. Questions that require solutions

9 Calculate: $\left(-2\frac{2}{3}\right)+\left(-4\frac{1}{3}\right)+6\frac{1}{2}$.

10 Calculate: $(-8.5)+\left(-10\frac{5}{6}\right)+\left(+\frac{5}{6}\right)$.

11 Calculate: $3\frac{1}{4}+\left(-2\frac{3}{5}\right)+5\frac{3}{4}+\left(-8\frac{2}{5}\right)$.

12 Calculate: $-2.4+3\frac{1}{3}+\left(-1\frac{1}{6}\right)+(-1.6)$.

13 There are 12 numbers on a clock face. The sum of the 12 numbers can be 0 by adding negative signs before some of the numbers, for example:
$(-1)+2+(-3)+4+(-5)+6+7+(-8)+9+(-10)+11+(-12)=0$.
(a) Write another equation using negative signs to make the sum of the 12 numbers 0.
(b) Think carefully. What is the minimum number of negative signs that should be added to make the sum 0?

2.5 Subtraction of rational numbers

Learning objective

Subtract rational numbers including both positive and negative numbers

A. Multiple choice questions

1 The following calculation that is equal to $3 - 7\frac{3}{5}$ is (   ).

A. $-\left(3 + 7\frac{3}{5}\right)$ B. $-3 - 7 + \frac{3}{5}$ C. $-\left(7\frac{3}{5} - 3\right)$ D. $7\frac{3}{5} - 3$

2 The following statement that is correct is (   ).

A. The sum of two rational numbers must be greater than one of the addends.

B. The sum of two rational numbers may be less than both of the addends.

C. The difference of two rational numbers must be less than the minuend.

> Note: If $a + b = c$, both a and b are called addends.
> If $a - b = c$, a is called the minuend and b is called the subtrahend.

D. The difference of a greater number minus a smaller number may be negative.

3 The sum of a number and $\left(-3\frac{3}{5}\right)$ is -0.36, then the number is (   ).

A. -2.24 B. -3.96 C. 3.24 D. 3.96

B. Fill in the blanks

4 Calculate.

(a) $10 - (-10) = $ _____   (b) $0 - (-5) = $ _____

(c) $0.9 - (-0.9) = $ _____   (d) $-66 - 66 = $ _____

(e) $8.9 - (+8.9) = $ _____   (f) $24 - (+12) = $ _____

5 The difference of $-\frac{6}{7}$ and $\frac{1}{7}$ is _____.

6 At the same time of day, the indoor temperature is $12.5°C$ and the outdoor temperature is $-4°C$. The outdoor temperature is _____ $°C$ lower than the indoor temperature.

7 Calculate: $-2\dfrac{3}{5}-\left(-3\dfrac{1}{4}\right)=$ _____.

8 If the sum of a number and the difference of 3 and $5\dfrac{3}{5}$ is 0, then the number is _____.

9 Calculate: $\left(-\dfrac{3}{4}\right)-\left(-\dfrac{1}{2}\right)-\left(+\dfrac{1}{8}\right)=$ _____.

 C. Questions that require solutions

10 Calculate: $0.32+\left(-3\dfrac{5}{6}\right)-\left(-\dfrac{17}{25}\right)-1\dfrac{1}{6}$.

11 Calculate: $13\dfrac{5}{6}-\left(-\dfrac{3}{4}\right)+\dfrac{5}{6}-\left(-\dfrac{7}{12}\right)$.

12 Calculate: $\left[1\dfrac{1}{2}-\left(3\dfrac{1}{2}-5\dfrac{2}{3}\right)-3\dfrac{2}{3}\right]-5$.

13 If the sum of $3\dfrac{1}{2}$ and the difference of a number and -0.4 is 0, find the number.

2.6 Multiplication of rational numbers (1)

Learning objective

Multiply rational numbers including both positive and negative numbers

A. Multiple choice questions

1 If the sum of two rational numbers is negative and their product is positive, then it is true that (   ).

A. one of them is positive and the other is negative

B. one of them is positive and the other is negative or zero

C. both are positive

D. both are negative

2 If $17a + 23b = 0$, then ab must be a (   ).

A. positive number   B. non-positive number

C. negative number   D. non-negative number

3 Among the following statements, (   ) is correct.

A. $-1\dfrac{1}{2} \times \dfrac{2}{3} = -1\dfrac{1}{3}$

B. $\left(-\dfrac{1}{2}\right) \times \left(-\dfrac{1}{2}\right) \times \left(-\dfrac{1}{2}\right) = \dfrac{1}{8}$

C. If the product of any number and -1 is added to the number itself, the result is 0.

D. The product of several numbers with the same sign is a non-negative number.

B. Fill in the blanks

4 If the product of three rational numbers is a positive number, there is/are at least _____ positive number(s) among the three.

5 Calculate: $-54 \times 2\dfrac{1}{6} =$ _____.

6 Calculate: $\left(-\dfrac{5}{12}\right) \times \left(-\dfrac{8}{15}\right) =$ _____.

7 Calculate: $\left(-\dfrac{5}{13}\right) \times \dfrac{13}{10} \times (-2) =$ _____.

8 The product of all integers that are greater than -3 but less than $4\dfrac{1}{3}$ is _____.

9 Without solving the equations, say whether x is positive or negative. Fill in each bracket with $+$ or $-$.

(a) $3x = -5$　　　　　(　　　)　　(b) $(-2) \times (-3)x = 10$　(　　　)

(c) $-\dfrac{5}{4} \times 11x = -0.6$　(　　　)　　(d) $\dfrac{4}{7} \times (-3 + x) = 1$　(　　　)

C. Questions that require solutions

10 Calculate: $\left(-3\dfrac{1}{5}\right) \times \left(+3\dfrac{3}{4}\right)$.

11 Calculate: $(-3) \times (-0.5) \times \left(-3\dfrac{1}{3}\right)$.

12 Calculate: $(-4) \times \left(+\dfrac{1}{2}\right) \times \left(-1\dfrac{2}{3}\right) \times \left(-2\dfrac{1}{4}\right)$.

13 Choose three numbers from 0.2, $-\dfrac{5}{8}$, -24 and 4, and find the greatest product of the three numbers. What is the least product of the three numbers?

2.7 Multiplication of rational numbers (2)

 Learning objective

Multiply rational numbers including both positive and negative numbers

A. Multiple choice questions

① Given that the sign of the product of 4 rational numbers is negative, there are
( ) positive numbers among the 4 numbers.

A. 1 or 3   B. 1 or 2   C. 2 or 4   D. 3 or 4

② If $-6 \times n \times m$ is negative and n is positive, the correct statement of the following
is ( ).

A. $m > 0$ B. $m \geqslant 0$ C. $m < 0$ D. $m \leqslant 0$

③ The correct statement of the following is ( ).

A. When multiplying several rational numbers, if the number of factors is an odd number, then the product is negative.

B. When multiplying several rational numbers, if the number of negative factors is an odd number, then the product is negative.

C. When multiplying several rational numbers, if the number of negative factors is an even number, then the product is positive.

D. When multiplying several rational numbers, if the product is negative, then the number of negative factors is an odd number.

 B. Fill in the blanks

④ Calculate: $\left(\dfrac{9}{10} - \dfrac{1}{15}\right) \times 30 = $ _____.

⑤ Calculate: $(-21) \times \left(1 + \dfrac{1}{3} - \dfrac{1}{21}\right) = $ _____.

⑥ Calculate: $\left(-\dfrac{7}{8}\right) \times 15 \times \left(-1\dfrac{1}{7}\right) = $ _____.

7 Fill in the blanks with $>$, $<$ or $=$.

(a) $(-3) \times (-5) \times (-7) \times (-9)$ _____ 0

(b) $(+3.86) \times (+2.9) \times (-7.98)$ _____ 0

(c) $831 \times (-123) \times (-239) \times 0$ _____ 0

8 Fill in the blanks with the laws of operations in mathematics that apply to the calculations below.

(a) $9.89 \times (-2.5) \times 4 = 9.89 \times [(-2.5) \times 4]$ _____

(b) $5\dfrac{5}{6} \times (-8) = 5 \times (-8) + \dfrac{5}{6} \times (-8)$ _____

C. Questions that require solutions

9 Calculate: $(-0.125) \times 15 \times (-8) \times \left(-\dfrac{4}{5}\right)$.

10 Calculate: $(-5.35) \times (-3) + 5.35 \times (-7) + 5.35 \times 4$.

11 Calculate: $\left(\dfrac{5}{12} - 2\dfrac{2}{3} - 1.75\right) \times (-24)$.

12 Calculate: $125 \times \left(-9\dfrac{24}{25}\right)$.

13 Find the product of $\frac{1}{4}$ of $3\frac{1}{5}$ and $\left(-\frac{5}{4}\right)$.

14 Complete following operations with the number 1000. First, subtract $\frac{1}{2}$ from it; second, subtract $\frac{1}{3}$ from the remaining number; third, subtract $\frac{1}{4}$ from the remaining number of the second subtraction. What is the remaining number after the 1000th operation?

2.8　Division of rational numbers

Learning objective

Divide rational numbers including both positive and negative numbers

A. Multiple choice questions

1 Among the following statements, the correct one is (　　).

A. The reciprocal of any number is less than or equal to 1.

B. The only number whose reciprocal is equal to the number itself is 1.

C. Dividing by a is the same as multiplying by $-a$.

D. Zero divided by any non-zero number is always zero.

2 Among the following calculations, the incorrect one is (　　).

A. $\frac{1}{3} \div (-3) = 3 \times (-3)$　　　　　B. $(-5) \div \left(-\frac{1}{2}\right) = -5 \times (-2)$

C. $8 - (-2) = 8 + 2$　　　　　D. $2 - 7 = (+2) + (-7)$

3 Among the following statements, (　　) of them is/are correct.

① The sum of two numbers must be greater than both of the two addends.

② The difference of two numbers must be less than the minuend.

③ The product of two numbers must be greater than the two factors.

④ The quotient of two numbers must be less than the dividend.

A. 0　　　　　B. 1　　　　　C. 2　　　　　D. 3

> Note: If $a \times b = c$, both a and b are called factors and c the product. If $a \div b = c$, a is called dividend, b is called divisor and c the quotient.

B. Fill in the blanks

4 The reciprocal of $-\frac{1}{25}$ is _____. The reciprocal of -2.25 is _____.

5 Calculate: $\left(-\frac{4}{3}\right) \div 6 = $ _____.

6 Calculate: $2\frac{1}{3} \div (-0.3) = $ _____.

7 Calculate: $-\frac{1}{2} \div \left(-1\frac{1}{2}\right) = $ _____.

8 Calculate: $\left(-2\frac{1}{7}\right) \div \left(+\frac{5}{14}\right) = $ _____.

9 $\frac{2}{5}$ of a number is -0.5. The number is _____.

 ## C. Questions that require solutions

10 Each number on the left is divided by $\left(-\frac{2}{3}\right)$. Write the answers in the corresponding places on the right.

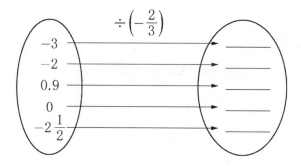

11 Calculate: $\left(-5\frac{1}{3}\right) \times \left(-2\frac{1}{4}\right) \div \left(-1\frac{1}{2}\right)$.

12 Calculate: $4.5 \div \left(-\dfrac{9}{8} \times \dfrac{4}{5} \right)$.

13 Calculate: $\left(-3\dfrac{1}{3} \right) \div 2\dfrac{4}{5} \div \left(-3\dfrac{1}{8} \right) \div (-0.75)$.

14 Read the solution to the example first, and then calculate:

$$\left(-\dfrac{1}{40} \right) \div \left(\dfrac{1}{2} - \dfrac{4}{5} + \dfrac{7}{8} - \dfrac{19}{20} \right).$$

Example

Calculate: $\left(-\dfrac{1}{24} \right) \div \left(\dfrac{1}{2} - \dfrac{2}{3} + \dfrac{3}{4} - \dfrac{5}{6} \right)$.

Solution: The reciprocal of the original expression is:

$$\left(\dfrac{1}{2} - \dfrac{2}{3} + \dfrac{3}{4} - \dfrac{5}{6} \right) \div \left(-\dfrac{1}{24} \right)$$

$$= \left(\dfrac{1}{2} - \dfrac{2}{3} + \dfrac{3}{4} - \dfrac{5}{6} \right) \times (-24)$$

$$= -12 + 16 - 18 + 20$$

$$= 6.$$

So: $\left(-\dfrac{1}{24} \right) \div \left(\dfrac{1}{2} - \dfrac{2}{3} + \dfrac{3}{4} - \dfrac{5}{6} \right) = \dfrac{1}{6}$.

2.9 Powers of rational numbers

Learning objective

Understand and use integer powers

A. Multiple choice questions

1 The value of 2^4 is (   ).

  A. 0   B. 6   C. 8   D. 16

2 -4^3 means (   ).

  A. 4 to the power 3   B. -4 to the power 3

  C. $-(4 \times 4 \times 4)$ D. none of the above

3 Given that rational number a is equal to its reciprocal, and the square of rational number b is zero, then $a^{2015} + b^{2015} = ($ $)$.

  A. 0   B. 1

  C. -1 D. ± 1 (i. e., 1 or -1)

4 Among the following pairs of numbers, the pair of numbers equal to each other is (   ).

  A. 3^2 and 2^3 B. -2^3 and $(-2)^3$

  C. -3^2 and $(-3)^2$ D. $2^3 \times 3^2$ and $(-2)^3 \times (-3)^2$

B. Fill in the blanks

5 To write $\left(\dfrac{1}{3}\right)^4$ using multiplication, it is _____. It is read as

_____. It can also be read as _____.

6 64 is the square of _____ and the cube of _____.

7 The base of a^4 is _____ and its

exponent is _____.

> When a number is expressed in the power form a^b, we call a the **base**, and b the **exponent**.

8 $\overbrace{(-2) \times (-2) \times (-2) \times \cdots \times (-2) \times (-2)}^{100 \text{ negative twos}}$ in the form of a power, it is _____ .

9 Calculate: $-0.5^3 =$ _____ .

10 Calculate: $-\left(-\dfrac{1}{3}\right)^2 =$ _____ .

C. Questions that require solutions

11 Put the numbers in order using $<$.

$$-\left(-\frac{2}{3}\right)^2 \qquad -\frac{2^2}{3} \qquad -\left(-\frac{2}{3}\right)^3 \qquad -\frac{2^3}{3}$$

12 Given $(2a+3)^2 + (b-2)^2 = 0$, find the value of a^b.

13 Given $(a-1)^4 + (2b+1)^4 = 0$, find the value of $a+2b$.

14 What is the least value of $(x+1)^2$ if x can be any number? When $(x+1)^2$ is the least, what number is x and therefore what value is x^{2015}?

2.10 Mixed operations of rational numbers (1)

 Learning objective

Use conventional notation for the priority of operations, including brackets and powers

 A. Multiple choice questions

1 If $a > 0$, $b < 0$, then $b - a$ must be a (   ).

A. positive number　　　　　　　B. negative number

C. non-positive number　　　　　D. all of the above are possible

2 In the results of the following calculations, (   ) of them is/are positive.

$$-5^2 \times 3,\ (3-5)^3 \times 3\frac{1}{4},\ (-3)^{98} - (-3)^{99},\ -\left(\frac{1}{2} - \frac{1}{3}\right) \times (-2)^3$$

A. 0　　　　　　B. 1　　　　　　C. 2　　　　　　D. 3

3 The result of $(-3) \times \frac{1}{3} \div \left(-\frac{1}{3}\right) \times 3$ is (   ).

A. 9　　　　　　B. -9　　　　　C. 1　　　　　D. -1

 B. Fill in the blanks

4 Calculate: $(4-3)^3 = $ _____.

5 Calculate: $4^3 - 3^3 = $ _____.

6 Calculate: $-(-3)^2 + (-2)^3 = $ _____.

7 Calculate: $-3^2 \div \frac{8}{27} \times \left(\frac{2}{3}\right)^2 = $ _____.

8 Calculate: $-5^2 - (-3)^3 \times \left(-\frac{2}{3}\right)^2 = $ _____.

C. Questions that require solutions

9 Are the following calculations correct? If not, write the correct solutions.

(a) $6 \div \left(\dfrac{1}{3} - \dfrac{1}{2} \right)$

$= 6 \div \dfrac{1}{3} - 6 \div \dfrac{1}{2}$

$= 6 \times 3 - 6 \times 2$

$= 18 - 12$

$= 6.$

(b) $-3^2 \div \dfrac{5}{9} \times 1\dfrac{4}{5}$

$= -3^2 \div \dfrac{5}{9} \times \dfrac{9}{5}$

$= -9 \div 1$

$= -9.$

10 Calculate: $-\dfrac{1}{2} - \left(-1\dfrac{1}{5} + 2\dfrac{7}{10} \right).$

11 Calculate: $4 \times (-3)^2 - 5 \times (-3) + 6.$

12 Calculate: $(-1.25) \times \dfrac{2}{5} \times 8 - 9 \div \left(-1\dfrac{1}{2} \right)^2.$

13 Calculate: $-3 \times 2^3 - [(-3) \times 2]^2 - (-2^3 \times 3)$.

14 Calculate: $(-2)^2 \times (+3) \div \left(-2\frac{2}{5}\right) - (-5)^2 \div 5 \times \left(-\frac{1}{5}\right)$.

2.11 Mixed operations of rational numbers (2)

 Learning objective

Use conventional notation for the priority of operations, including brackets and powers

 A. Multiple choice questions

① If $m > 0$ and $n < 0$, then the correct conclusion of the following is (   ).
A. $m + n > 0$ B. $m^2 - n^2 > 0$
C. $m^2 + n^3 > 0$ D. $m^3 + n^2 > 0$

② Among the following calculations, the correct one is (   ).
A. $-8 - 2 \times 6 = (-8 - 2) \times 6$ B. $2 \div \frac{4}{3} \times \frac{3}{4} = 2 \div \left(\frac{4}{3} \times \frac{3}{4} \right)$
C. $(-1)^{2001} + (-1)^{2002} = -1 + 1$ D. $-(-3^2) = -9$

③ If both $a + b$ and $a \times b$ are negative, then the following statement that is correct is
(   ).
A. a and b have the same sign and are both negative numbers.
B. a and b have the same sign and are both positive numbers.
C. a and b have different signs and $a > -b$.
D. a and b have different signs and $a < -b$.

B. Fill in the blanks

④ Calculate: $0 - (-3)^2 \div 3 \times (-2^3) = $ _____.

⑤ Calculate: $-16 \times \left(-\frac{7}{8} + \frac{3}{4} - \frac{1}{2} \right) \div (-5) = $ _____.

⑥ If $(-1)^n = 1$ and n is a positive integer, then n is an _____. If m is a
positive integer, then $(-1)^m + (-1)^{m+1} = $ _____.

⑦ If the sum of a and b is zero, c and d are reciprocal to each other, then $(-a-b)^{2016} + (cd)^{2017} = $ _____.

8 Calculate: $-2^2 + (-7) \div \left(-1\frac{3}{4}\right) = $ _____.

9 Calculate: $-2^3 \div \frac{4}{9} \times \left(-\frac{2}{3}\right)^3 = $ _____.

C. Questions that require solutions

10 Calculate: $\left[2\frac{1}{2} - \left(-\frac{1}{2}\right)^3\right] \times \left(-1\frac{1}{7}\right)$.

11 Calculate: $\left(-\frac{5}{8}\right) \times (-4^2) - 0.25 \times (-5) \times (-4)^3$.

12 Calculate: $54 \times 2\frac{1}{4} \div \left(-4\frac{1}{2}\right) \times \frac{2}{9}$.

13 Calculate: $1 - \frac{1}{2} \times \left[3 \times \left(-\frac{2}{3}\right)^2 - (-1)^4\right] + \frac{1}{4} \div \left(-\frac{1}{2}\right)^3$.

14 Given that $a = -1.8$, $b = -\frac{2}{3}$ and $c = 3$, find:

(a) $a - b - c$;

(b) $\frac{1}{a} + b^c$.

2.12 Expressing numbers in standard form

 Learning objective

Interpret and compare numbers in standard form

 A. Multiple choice questions

1 A 'light year' is a distance unit in astronomy. 1 light year is about $9\,500\,000\,000$ kilometres. In standard form, it can be written as (   ).

A. 9.5×10^8 km

B. 9.5×10^9 km

C. 9.5×10^{10} km

D. 9.5×10^{11} km

> Standard form, $A \times 10^n$ $(1 \leqslant A < 10)$, is also called 'scientific notation'.

2 In the following expressions, the correct one in standard form is (   ).

A. $254\,000 = 0.254 \times 10^6$ B. $254\,000 = 254 \times 10^3$

C. $254\,000 = 2.54 \times 10^3$ D. $254\,000 = 2.54 \times 10^5$

3 Given that N is a positive integer, then 10^N is (   ).

A. the product of ten Ns B. a N-digit integer

C. a $(N+1)$-digit integer   D. a $(N-2)$-digit integer

 B. Fill in the blanks

4 Express in standard form: $45\,600\,000 = $ _____ .

5 Express in standard form: 1.205 million pounds = _____ pounds.

6 Express in ordinary numbers: $-3.2 \times 10^7 = $ _____ .

7 If $a \times 10^n$ represents a 12-digit integer, $n = $ _____ .

8 The result of $3.2 \times 5 \times 10^7$ expressed in standard form is _____ .

C. Questions that require solutions

9 The total length of a high speed railway connecting Shanghai to the city's international airport is about 30 km and a single journey for a high speed train takes about 8 minutes. What is the average speed of the train per minute? Express your answer in standard form.

10 The on-orbit flight speed of a spacecraft was 7900 m per second, travelling one round of the Earth every 90 minutes. Approximately how many metres did the spacecraft move in travelling one round of the Earth? Express your answer in standard form.

11 Put the numbers 7.91×10^6, 1.2×10^7, 8.3×10^6, 2.3×10^7, 0.07×10^8 in order, starting from the least.

12 Let's explore.

(a) 10^2 stands for the multiplication of _____ 10s and 10^3 stands for the multiplication of _____ 10s, therefore $10^2 \times 10^3$ stands for the multiplication of _____ 10s and the product is 10 to the power _____ .

(b) 10^m stands for the multiplication of _____ 10s and 10^n stands for the multiplication of _____ 10s, therefore $10^m \times 10^n$ stands for the multiplication of _____ 10s and the product is 10 to the power _____ .

(c) Using the pattern obtained above, calculate: $1.25 \times 10^{11} \times 8 \times 10^{10}$.

Unit test 2

1 The altitudes of places A, B and C are 20 m, -15 m and -10 m, respectively. The difference between the highest place and the lowest place is (   ).

A. 5 m

B. 10 m

C. 15 m

D. 35 m

2 Among the numbers 10.1, $-(-5)$, -0.5, 10%, 0, 2, $(-1)^3$, -2^2 and $-(-2)^2$, there are (   ) non-negative numbers.

A. 4

B. 5

C. 6

D. 7

3 The following pair of numbers that are equal are (   ).

A. $(-4)^2$ and -4^2

B. $(-3)^7$ and -3^7

C. $(2-1)^2$ and 2^2-1^2

D. $(-2)^8$ and -2^8

4 If the ordinary number of 2.05×10^n is a 14-digit integer, then the value of n is (   ).

A. 12

B. 13

C. 14

D. 15

5 If $a > 0$, $b < 0$ and a is less than $-b$, then the correct expression of the following is (   ).

A. $-b > a > -a > b$

B. $b > a > -b > -a$

C. $-b > a > b > -a$

D. $a > b > -a > -b$

6 Among the following statements, the correct one is (   ).

A. If $a^2 > b^2$, then $a > b$

B. If $a > b$, then $a^2 > b^2$

C. If $a^2 = b^2$, then $a = b$

D. If $a = b$, then $a^2 = b^2$

B. Fill in the blanks

7 If a number added to -3 is zero, then the number is _____ .

8 If a point on a number line has a distance of 4 from the point which represents $-2\frac{3}{5}$, then the number the point represents on the line is _____ .

9 Express in standard form: $-32\ 500\ 000 =$ _____ .

10 Compare the numbers: 1^{2000} _____ $(-1)^{2001}$.

11 $-1\frac{1}{2} +$ _____ $= -2\frac{1}{6}$

12 Calculate: $-2\frac{1}{7} \times 1.2 \div \left(-1\frac{2}{5}\right) =$ _____ .

13 Calculate: $(-3)^2 \times \frac{1}{6} =$ _____ .

14 Calculate: $\left(-2\frac{4}{25}\right) \times 75 =$ _____ .

15 Choose any three numbers from -2, -3, -4 and 5, then multiply. The least possible product is _____ .

16 The temperatures recorded on two winter days in a city are shown in the table.

	Highest temperature	Lowest temperature
First day	9.1	2.3
Second day	5.2	-2.3

In the two days, the _____ day had greater temperature difference between the highest and the lowest.

17 If $a^2 = 25$, $b = -2$, $ab > 0$, then $a + b =$ _____ .

18 If $(x+3)^2 = 0$, then $x =$ _____

19 Follow the steps below, if the value of the output is $-\dfrac{1}{9}$, then the value of the input x is _____ .

$$\boxed{\text{input } x} \longrightarrow \boxed{\text{minus 5}} \longrightarrow \boxed{\text{square}} \longrightarrow \boxed{\text{negative reciprocal}} \longrightarrow \boxed{\text{output}}$$

C. Questions that require solutions

20 Calculate: $0.5 + \left(-\dfrac{1}{4}\right) - (-2.75) + \left(+\dfrac{1}{2}\right)$.

21 Calculate: $(-24) \times \left(\dfrac{5}{3} - 3\dfrac{1}{2} + 1\dfrac{7}{8}\right)$.

22 Calculate: $\left(-\dfrac{5}{8} - \dfrac{7}{12}\right) \div 4\dfrac{5}{6} - \left(-\dfrac{3}{4}\right)$.

23 Calculate: $0.25 \times (-2)^3 - \left[4 \div \left(-\dfrac{2}{3}\right)^2 + 1\right]$.

24 What is the difference between the cube of $-\dfrac{1}{2}$ and the square of $-\dfrac{3}{4}$?

25 In testing the mass of 5 basketballs, the amount of mass (unit: g) exceeding the standard mass is recorded as positive and that below the standard mass is recorded as negative. The outcome of the testing is shown in the table.

Number label of each basketball	1	2	3	4	5
Difference from the standard mass (unit: gram)	+4	+7	−3	−8	+9

(a) The basketball that is closest to the standard mass is basketball number _____ .

(b) How many grams heavier is the heaviest basketball than the lightest basketball?

26 Given that the three points on a number line corresponding to the three rational numbers are $A: -2\dfrac{1}{5}$, $B: \dfrac{7}{10}$ and $C: x$, if $AC = 3BC$, find the value of x.

Chapter 3   Linear equations

3.1   Establishing simple equations

Learning objective

Understand and use concepts of equations and related terms

A. Multiple choice questions

1 In the following equations, the one that does not involve a variable is (　　).

A. $x = -3$

B. $4 + 3 = 7$

C. $x^2 + 1 = 0$

D. $2x - y = 7$

> A **variable** in an equation is an unknown number. It is also simply called an **unknown**.

2 In the following, there are (　　) equations with one variable.

① $2x^2 + 1 = 3x - 4$　② $5y - 1 = 0$　③ $6x^2 = -1$　④ $2t + 1 = 4$

A. 1　　　　　　B. 2　　　　　　C. 3　　　　　　D. 4

B. Fill in the blanks

3 In solving a problem, to establish an equation is to set up an _____ relationship between known numbers and unknown numbers. (Choose 'equal' or 'unequal' to fill in the blank.)

4 In the equation $\frac{3}{2}xy - x = 0$, the coefficient in the term '$-x$' is _____.

The degree of the term $\frac{3}{2}xy$ is _____.

> The **degree** of a term is the sum of the exponents of all the variables.

5 Fill in the table.

	$2x$	$5^2 m^3$	$-\dfrac{4}{7}x^2 y$	$m^2 n^3$
Coefficient				
Degree				

C. Questions that require solutions

6 In each question below, establish an equation based on the given conditions. (Choose a suitable letter to represent the unknown number.)

(a) A number is $\dfrac{5}{16}$ greater than $\dfrac{4}{5}$ of the number.

(b) $\dfrac{4}{5}$ of a number is $\dfrac{5}{16}$ greater than the number itself.

7 Establish an equation using the quantitative relationship given.

(a) The sum of 2 times x and 3 is 11.

(b) The difference between 12 and x squared is 8.

(c) x is 4 greater than its reciprocal.

8 Using the formula you have learned, establish an equation with a suitable variable for each question below.

(a) Given that the diameter of a circle is 64 cm, find its radius.

(b) The length of a rectangle is 3 times the width. Its perimeter is 48 cm. Find the width of the rectangle.

9 Mr Kelly needed to allocate a large group of students into dormitories. He found that if 4 students shared one dormitory, there would be 5 dormitories left unoccupied. If 3 students shared one dormitory, there would be 100 students left unallocated. How many students were there? Help Mr Kelly establish an equation with a suitable variable.

3.2 Solutions to equations

Learning objective

Substitute numerical values into equations to establish if they are solutions

A. Multiple choice questions

1. $x = 2$ is the solution to the equation (   ).

    A. $\dfrac{1}{2}x + 3 = 5$

    B. $-\dfrac{1}{3}x + 7 = 6x$

    C. $5x - 8 = 2$

    D. $\dfrac{1}{4}x + 5 = 9$

> A **solution** to an equation is a value that, when substituted for the variable, makes the equation true.

2. $x = \dfrac{1}{2}$ is not the solution to the equation (   ).

    A. $x + 1 = 1\dfrac{1}{2}$

    B. $2x^2 + 10 = 10.5$

    C. $-2x + 7 = 6$

    D. $4x + \dfrac{1}{2} = 4\dfrac{1}{2}$

B. Fill in the blanks

3. A value that makes an equation true when it is substituted for the variable is called a _____ to the equation.

4. $k = 0$ _____ a solution to the equation $k + 1 = -k + 1$. (Choose 'is' or 'is not' to fill in.)

5. $n = 1$ _____ a solution to the equation $3n - 9 = 6$. (Choose 'is' or 'is not' to fill in.)

6. $x = 1$ _____ a solution to the equation $4x^2 - 9 = 2x - 7$. (Choose 'is' or 'is not' to fill in.)

7 $x = 2$ _____ a solution to the equation $\dfrac{x^2 - 2}{x} - \dfrac{3x}{x^2 - 2} + 2 = 0$. (Choose 'is' or 'is not' to fill in.)

8 If the solutions to the equations $3x + 8 = 2$ and $2x - a = 4x + 3$ are reciprocal to each other, then a must be _____.

9 If $x = 2$ is the solution to the equation $ax - 1 = 0$, then a must be _____ and $x = 4$ _____ a solution to the equation $2ax + x - 7 = 0$. (Choose 'is' or 'is not' to fill in.)

C. Questions that require solutions

10 Check whether each of the following numbers is a solution to the equation $x^2 - 3 = 2x$.

① $x = -1$ ② $x = -3$ ③ $x = 3$ ④ $x = 1$

11 Write one equation for each value of x below, so the value of x is a solution to the equation.

(a) $x = -\dfrac{1}{2}$ (b) $x = 1$ (c) $x = 2$

12 What value should k take so that $x = 2$ is a solution to the equation $kx = x^2 - x + 1$?

13 (a) Are both $x = 1$ and $x = -1$ solutions to the equation $x^2 - 1 = 0$? Explain why.

(b) Write an equation so that both $x = 3$ and $x = -3$ are solutions to the equation.

3.3 Linear equations in one variable and their solution (1)

 Learning objective

Solve linear equations with one unknown

 A. Multiple choice questions

1 Which of the following equations is a linear equation in one variable? (   )

A. $5x = 0$

B. $x + 2 = x^2$

C. $2y - (x + 9) = 15$

D. $\dfrac{1}{x} + 1 = 2$

2 Which of the following shows a correct transposition of a term from one side of the equation to the other side? (   )

A. From $5 + x = 8$, we can get $x = 5 + 8$.

B. From $5x = 2x - 3$, we can get $5x - 2x = 3$.

C. From $7x = 8x - 2$, we can get $7x - 8x = -2$.

D. From $x - 5 = 4x + 2$, we can get $x + 2 = 4x + 5$.

> To **transpose** a term from one side of an equation to the other, we change the sign of the term and keep everything else unchanged. (Do you know why it works?)

 B. Fill in the blanks

3 The equation $2x - 1 = 3$ is a _____ equation with _____ variable(s).

4 The equation $\dfrac{1}{2}x + \dfrac{1}{3}y = 0$ is a _____ equation with _____ variable(s).

5 The solution to the equation $2x - 9 = 15 - x$ is _____.

6 The equation $2x - 3 = 3x - x + 2$ has _____ solution.

C. Questions that require solutions

7 Solve the following equations.

(a) $x + 12 = 34$ (b) $5x = -2x + 14$

8 Solve the following equations.

(a) $2x + 5 = 25 - 8x$ (b) $9 + 11y = 10y - 7\dfrac{1}{3}$

9 Solve the equation: $1 - 8\left(\dfrac{x}{4} - \dfrac{5}{2}\right) = 5x$

10 Given $3x^{n+1} + 2x - 7 = 8$ is a linear equation for x and n is a non-negative number, find the value of n and hence the solution to the equation.

11 Given a is a known number, for what value of a is the equation $a^2 x^2 - x^2 + 2x - 2ax - 3 = 0$ a linear equation for x?

3.4 Linear equations in one variable and their solution (2)

Learning objective

Solve linear equations with unknowns on both sides

A. Multiple choice questions

1. Which of the following shows the correct result of removing the brackets from the expression on the left of each equation? (   )

   A. $1-3(x+1) = 1-3x-1$

   B. $1-3\left(\frac{1}{3}x-1\right) = 1-x+3$

   C. $1-2\left(x-\frac{1}{2}\right) = 1-2x-1$

   D. $5(x-2)-2(3y-1) = 5x-10-6y-2$

2. Let a number be x. If 1 greater than $\frac{3}{4}$ of x is -5, then we can establish the equation (   ).

   A. $-\frac{3}{4}x+1 = 5$ 　　　　　　 B. $-\left(\frac{3}{4}x+1\right) = 5$

   C. $\frac{3}{4}x-1 = 5$ 　　　　　　　 D. $-x\left(\frac{3}{4}x+1\right) = 5$

B. Fill in the blanks

3. Removing the brackets from $-3(x-2) = 12$, it is _____ .

4. Removing the brackets from $5(x+2) = -2(2x-7)$, it is _____ .

5. The solution to the equation $5(x-2) = 7$ is _____ .

C. Questions that require solutions

Solve the following equations.

6 $2x - 6 = 3x - 5(x - 2)$

7 $3(x - 4) - 2(4x - 3) = 12(x - 9)$

8 $x - 2[x - 3(x + 4) - 6] = 1$

9 $2(x - 2) - 3(4x - 1) = 9(1 - x)$

10 $7(2x - 1) - 3(3x + 5) + 1 = 2(9x - 4)$

11 $5(x - 4) - 7(7 - x) - 9 = 12 - 3(9 - x)$

12 $3x - [5(x + 2) - (x - 6)] = 4x + 7$

3.5 Linear equations in one variable and their solution (3)

 Learning objective

Solve linear equations with unknowns on both sides, including fractions

 A. Multiple choice questions

1 To remove the denominators in the equation $\frac{x+1}{2} + \frac{x-1}{3} - 2 = \frac{2x+1}{6}$, both

sides of the equation should be multiplied by (   ).

A. 2　　　　　　B. 3　　　　　　C. 6　　　　　　D. 12

2 To remove the denominators in the equation $\frac{5x-2}{8} - \frac{3x-1}{6} = \frac{x+1}{6} - \frac{1-x}{3}$,

both sides of the equation should be multiplied by (   ).

A. 3　　　　　　B. 6　　　　　　C. 8　　　　　　D. 24

3 To remove the denominators in the equation $\frac{3x-1}{2} - \frac{5-2x}{3} = \frac{5x+3}{4} - 2$, both

sides of the equation should be multiplied by (   ).

A. 2　　　　　　B. 3　　　　　　C. 4　　　　　　D. 12

 B. Fill in the blanks

4 Solve the equation: $\frac{7x-5}{4} = \frac{3}{8}$.

Solution: Remove the denominators: _____.

(Note: multiplying both sides by the lowest common multiple or LCM)

Remove the brackets: _____.

Transpose the term _____ from LHS to RHS: _____.

(RHS/LHS: Right-hand side/Left-hand side)

Simplify: _____.

Divided both sides by _____ and get: _____.

So the solution to the original equation is _____.

⑤ The solution to the equation $\dfrac{5-3x}{2} = \dfrac{3-5x}{3}$ is _____.

⑥ The solution to the equation $\dfrac{x}{5} - \dfrac{3-2x}{2} = x$ is _____.

C. Questions that require solutions

Solve the following equations.

⑦ $\dfrac{x-2}{5} - \dfrac{x+3}{10} - \dfrac{2x-5}{3} + 3 = 0$

⑧ $\dfrac{2}{3}x - \dfrac{3}{2}\left(1 - \dfrac{3-x}{3}\right) = \dfrac{2-3x}{6}$

⑨ $\dfrac{1}{3}\left(3x - \dfrac{10-7x}{2}\right) - \dfrac{1}{2}\left(2x - \dfrac{2x+2}{3}\right) = \dfrac{x}{2} - 1$

⑩ $\dfrac{10}{63}(3x+6) + \dfrac{2}{21}(x+2) + \dfrac{3}{14}(2x+4) = 1$

11 $\dfrac{0.4x+0.9}{0.5} - \dfrac{0.03+0.02x}{0.03} = \dfrac{x-5}{2}$

12 $\dfrac{x}{0.25} - \dfrac{x+1}{0.4} = \dfrac{x-5}{0.2} - 2$

3.6　Application of linear equations in one variable (1)

Learning objective

Solve linear equations with real life situations

A. Multiple choice questions

1. Amy had £16. She used it to buy some stamps with values of 80p and £1. Given that the number of £1 stamps is 2 fewer than the number of 80p stamps, and let the number of 80p stamps be x, then the equation that satisfies the given conditions is (　　).

   A. $0.8x + (x-2) = 16$　　　　　　B. $0.8x + (x+2) = 16$

   C. $80x + (x-2) = 16$　　　　　　D. $80x + (x+2) = 16$

2. A school library bought 32 maths books and 18 science books in March. In April, it bought another 20 books in maths and science. As a result, the library bought twice as many maths books as science books in the two months. How many maths books did the library buy in April? How many science books did it buy in April? To solve the above problem, let the number of maths books it bought in April be x, then the correct equation of the following is (　　).

   A. $32 + x = 2 \times 18$　　　　　　B. $32 + x = 2(18 + 20 - x)$

   C. $52 - x = 2(18 + x)$　　　　　　D. $52 - x = 2 \times 18$

B. Fill in the blanks

3. A car manufacturer produced a cars in one month and the production in the following month was x % more than that in the first month. The total number of cars produced in the two months was _____.

4. A test consists of 20 questions. Five marks are awarded for each correct answer, 0 marks are awarded if no answer is given, and -1 mark is awarded for each incorrect answer. If Jim left 3 questions unanswered and he got 79 marks, then he answered _____ questions correctly.

C. Questions that require solutions

(For each question below, establish a suitable linear equation and then solve the problem.)

5 A health survey is conducted in a school. 120 students were chosen from Years 7, 8 and 9 in a ratio of 4 : 5 : 3. How many students were chosen in each year group?

6 A messenger cycles to an office to deliver a document within a specified amount of time. If he cycles at 15 km/h, then he will reach the office 25 minutes earlier. If he cycles at 12 km/h, then he will reach there 12 minutes later. What is the specified amount of time? What is the distance between the messenger's starting point and the office?

7 A ship sailed down from Dock A and after 5 hours it arrived at Dock B. When the ship sailed back along the same route, it took 6 hours. Given that the current of water was 2 km/h, find the speed of the ship in still waters.

8 There are two options for the installment of payment for purchasing a refrigerator. Option 1: Pay £750 for the first month and thereafter £150 for each month. Option 2: Pay £300 per month for the first half of the installment period and £100 per month for the other half of the installment period. If the total amount and the duration of the payment are the same under both options, find the total cost of the refrigerator.

3.7 Application of linear equations in one variable (2)

Learning objective

Solve linear equations with real life situations

A. Multiple choice questions

1 Given the cost price of an item is x pounds and the profit is 15%, the selling price is (   ).

A. $0.15x$ B. $x + 15x$ C. $x + 0.15x$ D. $x - 0.15x$

2 If the cost price of an item is £180 and the selling price is x pounds, then the percentage of the profit is (   ).

A. $\frac{x-180}{180}\%$ B. $\frac{x-180}{180} \times 100\%$ C. $\frac{180-x}{180}\%$ D. $\frac{180-x}{180} \times 100\%$

B. Fill in the blanks

3 Given that a set of sportswear is sold at £135, which is 25% less than the original selling price, the original price was £_____ .

4 The cost price of a pair of leather shoes was x pounds and the regular selling price was set 50% higher than the cost price. Later, in a seasonal promotion a discount of 25% was offered and the shoes were priced at £31.50. The cost price was _____ pounds.

5 If the perimeter of a rectangle is 25 cm and its length is twice its width, then the length is _____ cm.

C. Questions that require solutions

(For each question below, establish a suitable linear equation and then solve the problem.)

6 The length of a rectangular swimming pool is 3 m longer than twice its width. If its perimeter is 72 m, what are its length and width?

7 A shop set the selling price of a certain brand of clothes at 40% more than its cost price. Later, in a promotion, it sold the clothes at a 20% discount but the profit was £15 for each set of the clothes sold. What was the cost price?

8 To complete a task, it will take Avin 15 days and Bob 30 days if they work individually. Given that Avin first worked on the task for 5 days and after that Bob continued to work on it for 10 days, how many more days are still needed to complete the rest of the work if the remaing work is to be completed by them jointly?

9 Team A can complete a project in 20 days while Team B can complete it in 30 days. Team A started working on a project for 6 days. After that, $\frac{4}{15}$ of the team members left the project for another task, and Team B joined the remaining members of Team A to complete the project together. How many more days did they need to complete it?

10 An electrical store set the regular selling price of a brand of computer at 35% above the cost price, and then sold it under the promotion '10% off plus extra £50 cash back'. In the end, the shop has still made a profit of £208 from each computer sold. What was the cost price of each computer?

Unit test 3

A. Multiple choice questions

1. In transforming the equation $\frac{1}{2}(x-1)=\frac{1}{5}x+1$, the incorrect one of the following is (   ).

   A. Remove the denominator: $5(x-1)=2x+1$

   B. Remove the bracket: $\frac{1}{2}x-\frac{1}{2}=\frac{1}{5}x+1$

   C. Transpose the terms: $\frac{1}{2}x-\frac{1}{5}x=\frac{1}{2}+1$

   D. Rearrange: $\frac{1}{2}(x-1)=\frac{1}{5}(x+5)$

2. In the following equations, the one that has the solution $x=3$ is (   ).

   A. $\frac{x-3}{2}+\frac{x-2}{3}=1$ B. $5(3-2x)=3(x+2)$

   C. $x-4=\frac{1-x}{2}$ D. $x-\frac{1-x}{2}=2$

3. If $(a-1)^2+2(b+3)^2=0$, then the value of $\frac{b}{a}+1$ is (   ).

   A. -2 B. -3 C. -4 D. 4

4. The sum of three numbers is 6. When the first number has 1 added to it and the second number has 1 subtracted from it, both answers are equal to the third number. The product of the three numbers is (   ).

   A. 6   B. 3   C. 2   D. 8

B. Fill in the blanks

5. The solution to the equation $5x-1=2(x-5)$ is _____.

6 If the equation $(m+2)x^2 + 3mx - 4m = 0$ for x is a linear equation with one variable, then the solution to the equation is _____ .

7 If $\dfrac{2x+1}{3}$ and $-\dfrac{3}{2}$ are reciprocals to each other, then the value of x is _____ .

8 A batch of spare parts is to be made. If 50 spare parts are to be made each day, the batch of spare parts will be made 8 days later than the original plan. If 60 spare parts are to be made each day, this batch will be made 5 days ahead of the original plan. How many spare parts are there in this batch?

9 If when $x = 1$, $3 - ax = 5$, then when $x = -1$, $3 - ax = $ _____ .

10 Establish an equation with the given condition: the difference between x squared and $\dfrac{2}{5}$ of x is the reciprocal of -2: _____ .

C. Questions that require solutions

11 Solve the equation: $2(x+3) = 15 - x$.

12 Solve the equation: $-\dfrac{x-3}{2} + \dfrac{5-2x}{4} = -2 + \dfrac{x-2}{8}$.

⑬ Solve the equation: $\frac{1}{2}\left[\frac{4}{3}x-\left(\frac{2}{3}x-\frac{1}{2}\right)\right]=\frac{3}{4}x.$

⑭ Solve the equation: $\dfrac{1+\frac{1}{3}x}{2}=\dfrac{0.1x-0.05}{0.3}+\dfrac{1}{6}.$

(Note: For each question below, establish a suitable linear equation and then solve the problem.)

⑮ The perimeter of a rectangular garden is 184 m. Its length is 10 metres longer than three times the width. What is the length and the width of the rectangular garden?

⑯ Tom and Jack needed to go from one place to another place. Tom's speed was 6 km/h and Jack's speed was 5 km/h. If Tom started 15 minutes later than Jack, but reached the destination 1 hour earlier, then the distance between the two places was _____ km.

17 Some rooms are to be allocated to some trainees. If 4 trainees share one room, there will be 19 trainees left without rooms. If 6 trainees share one room, there will be only 5 trainees left for the last room. Find the number of rooms and the number of trainees.

18 Taxi fares in a city are charged as follows: a flat rate of £12 is charged for the first 3 km or shorter distance; from 3 km up to 10 km, the rate is £2.40 per km; and over 10 km it is £3.60 per km. One day, Mr Lee took a taxi to a community centre and he paid £32.40 for the taxi fare. How many kilometres did he travel in the taxi? (Ignore the waiting time charge.)

Chapter 4　Line segments, angles and circles

4.1　Line segments and their lengths

Learning objective

Understand and use conventions and notations for lines and line segments

A. Multiple choice questions

1 Among the following pairs of items, comparing lengths is only meaningful for items in (　　).

A. two lines

B. a line and a line segment

C. two line segments

D. none of the above

A **straight line** (or simply a **line**) has no beginning point or endpoint in both directions. A **line segment** (or simply a **segment**) is part of a line with two endpoints in both directions.

2 As shown in the diagram, the correct statement below is (　　).

A. Point A is on segment BO.

B. Point A is not on line BO.

C. Point A is on the extension of segment BO beyond O.

D. Point A is on the extension of segment BO beyond B.

Diagram for question 2

3 The distance between points A and B means (　　).

A. the line segment joining A and B

B. the line passing through points A and B

C. the length of line AB

D. the length of the line segment joining A and B

4 The correct statement of the following is (　　).

A. Between line segments and lines, lines are longer.

B. The length of a line is twice the length of a segment.

C. Line AB means the distance between points A and B.

D. If point C is on the line segment AB, then $AB \geqslant CB$.

B. Fill in the blanks

5 A line segment can be denoted by _____ capital letter(s) or _____ small letter(s). (Choose 'one' or 'two' to fill in.)

6 In all the routes connecting two points, the line segment is the _____ in terms of the distance. (Choose 'shortest' or 'longest' to fill in.)

7 The distance between two points refers to the length of _____ that joins them.

8 The diagram shows _____ line segments. They are
_____ , and the longest segment is _____.
From points A to B, the shortest route is _____ and
the reason is _____ .

Diagram for question 8

9 A line segment has _____ endpoint(s) and a line has _____ endpoint(s).

10 As shown in the diagram, there are three separate points, A, B and C on line l. There are _____ line segments.

Diagram for question 10

C. Questions that require solutions

11 Draw the diagrams with the conditions given.

(a) Point A is on line a and point B is outside line a.

(b) Lines a and b intersect at point M.

(c) Lines a and b intersect at point A and lines b and c intersect at point B.

12 Draw the diagram with the given conditions.

(a) Extend AD beyond D to point E, so that $ED = AD$.

(b) Connect BD.

(c) Connect AC and extend AC beyond C so it intersects BD at O.

(d) Extend BC beyond B to M, so that $MC = 2MB$.

(e) Use a ruler to mark BD's midpoint F.

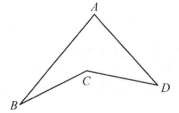

Diagram for question 12

13 First, write the number of line segments in the following diagrams and then answer the questions below.

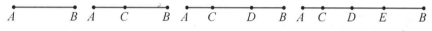

No. of segments: _____   _____   _____   _____

(a) Based on the diagrams above, make a guess: when there are 10 points on the line segment AB (excluding A and B points), how many segments will there be?

(b) How many segments are there if there are n points on the segment (excluding both endpoints)?

4.2 Constructing line segments, their sums and differences

Learning objective

Construct line segments and their midpoints

A. Multiple choice questions

1. The following statement that is correct is (   ).
   A. The distances between the midpoint of a segment and the two endpoints are equal.
   B. If $OA = OB$, then O is the midpoint of the segment AB.
   C. A line segment may have more than one midpoint.
   D. The route mileage from Leeds to Edinburgh by train is about 345 km. It means that the distance between the two cities is also about 345 km.

2. There are three points, A, B and C on a plane. Given $AB = 8$ cm and $BC = 5$ cm, then AC is (   ).
   A. 13 cm
   B. 3 cm
   C. 13 cm or 3 cm
   D. not sure

3. Point C is on the line segment AB of length 30 cm. The distance between the midpoint of AC and the midpoint of BC is (   ).
   A. 11 cm
   B. 15 cm
   C. 12 cm
   D. 13 cm

4. As shown in the diagram, if there is a point C on the line AB to make $AC = 2CB$, then C is (   ).
   A. between A and B
   B. on the left side of A
   C. on the left side of B
   D. between A and B or on the right side of B

   A ————————————— B

   Diagram for question 4

B. Fill in the blanks

5 Two line segments can be added or subtracted and their sum or difference is also a
_____ . Its length is either _____ or _____ of the lengths of the
two segments.

6 As shown in the diagram, $AD = AB + $ _____ ,
$AD - BD = $ _____ , $CD = AD - $ _____ $- $ _____ .

A B   C D

Diagram for question 6

7 Given segment $AB = 10$ cm and M is the midpoint of AB, then $AM = $ _____ cm.

8 If M is the midpoint of segment AB, then $AM = $ _____ $= \dfrac{1}{2}$ _____ ,
$AB = 2$ _____ $= 2$ _____ .

9 As shown in the diagram, D is the midpoint of the
segment AB. If $CD = \dfrac{1}{2}AC$ and $CD = 3$ cm, then
$AB = $ _____ cm.

A   C   D   B

Diagram for question 9

10 Given $AB = 2$ cm, if AB is extended beyond B to point C so $BC = AB$ and beyond
A to point D so $AD = AB$, then $AC = $ _____ cm, $BD = $ _____ cm. (Hint:
draw a diagram to help.)

11 If point C divides the segment AB into two parts in the ratio of $2 : 5$ and
$BC = 1.5$ cm, then $AB = $ _____ cm.

12 Given point C is on the segment AB, and D and E are the midpoints of the
segments AC and BC respectively, then $DE = $ _____ AB.

13 Segment $AB = 6$ cm. If AB is extended beyond B to point C so $BC = 3$ cm, then AC
is _____ times BC.

14 On a given line l, if we take a segment $AB = 5$ cm and again take segment
$BC = 2$ cm, then the length of the segment AC is _____ cm.

C. Questions that require solutions

15 As shown in the diagram, segment AB is divided by point M in the ratio of $2 : 3$ and divided by point N in the ratio of $1 : 4$. Given that $MN = 3$ cm, find the length of AB.

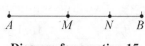

Diagram for question 15

16 Given point C is the midpoint of segment AB, point D is the midpoint of segment AC, point E is the midpoint of segment CB, and $AB = 10$ cm, find the lengths of segments AE and DE.

17 Given segments a and b, use a ruler and compasses to construct segment MN so that $MN = 2a - b$.

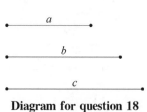

Diagram for question 17

18 Given segments a, b and c, use a ruler and compasses to construct segment AB so that $AB = a + \dfrac{1}{2}b - c$.

a

b

c

Diagram for question 18

19 Construct a segment AB and take a point C on the extension of AB beyond B, so that $BC = 2AB$. P is the midpoint of BC. If $AB = 3$ cm, find the length of BP.

4.3 Angle concepts and representations

 Learning objective

Label and identify angles using standard notation

A. Multiple choice questions

1 In the diagram, there is/are (   ) angle(s).

A. 0   B. 1

C. 3   D. 5

Diagram for question 1

2 Among the following statements, the correct one is (   ).

A. A straight angle can be divided into two acute angles.

B. The two sides of a straight angle are on the same line.

C. Two right angles with a common endpoint form a straight angle.

D. None of the above is correct.

3 In the diagram, to represent an angle with D as the vertex,

the correct one of the following is (   ).

A. $\angle ADE$ B. $\angle DAE$

C. $\angle D$ D. $\angle AED$

Diagram for question 3

4 If the direction of point B from point A is $30°$ east of north, then the direction of point A from point B is (   ).

A. $60°$ east of south   B. $60°$ west of south

C. $30°$ east of south   D. $30°$ west of south

B. Fill in the blanks

5 An angle has _____ vertex and _____ sides. The point at which the two sides meet is called the _____ of the angle.

6 In general, an angle can be denoted by _____. It can also be denoted by ____

_____.

7 In terms of transformation, an angle can also be viewed as the figure formed by a _____ of part of a line with one endpoint (or called a ray) around the endpoint from one position to another position. (Choose 'rotation', or 'translation', or 'reflection' to fill in.)

8 In terms of rotation, the initial side of the angle shown in the diagram is _____, the terminal side is _____ and the vertex of the angle is _____.

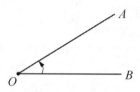

Diagram for question 8

9 As shown in the diagram, point C is _____ $\angle AOB$, point D is _____ $\angle AOB$ and point E is _____ $\angle AOB$. (Choose 'on', or 'inside', or 'outside' to fill in.)

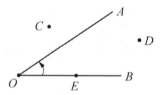

Diagram for question 9

10 Use the correct notation to represent each angle shown in the diagram.

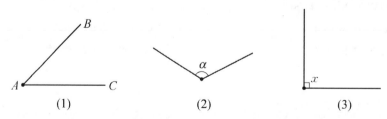

Diagram for question 10

(1) _____ (2) _____ (3) _____

11 At 9 a.m., the angle between the hour hand and the minute hand on a clock is _____ degrees. At 6 p.m., it is _____ degrees. At 4 p.m., it is _____ degrees.

12 As shown in the diagram, _____ is an acute angle, _____
_____ is a right angle, _____ is an obtuse angle. There are _____ angles
less than 180°.
They are _____ .

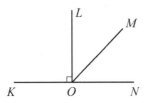

Diagram for question 12

C. Questions that require solutions

13 Look at the diagram, and indicate the directions of
OA, OB, OC and OD, all starting from O. The first one
has been done for you.

OA: 10° east of north*

OB: _____

OC: _____

OD: _____

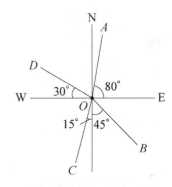

Diagram for question 13

14 Look at each diagram and shade the exterior area of the angle marked β.

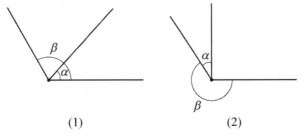

(1)   (2)

Diagram for question 14

---

* We usually use $x°$ east (or west) of north (or south) to describe the direction of a point A from
another point B, where x must be an acute angle. If x is zero, then the direction is due north or
south, if x is 90 then it is due east or west, and if x is 45, then it is called northeast, or southeast,
northwest, or southwest, all depending on the location of A in relation to B. In this case, A is in
the direction of 10° east of north from point O.

15 Look at the diagram and represent the angles as indicated.

(a) all the angles with C as the vertex

(b) all the angles with AB as one side

(c) all the angles with F as the vertex and FB as one side

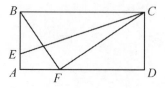

Diagram for question 15

16 Count the number of the angles that are less than a straight angle in the diagram. There are _____ such angles.

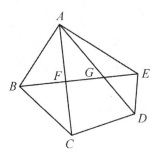

Diagram for question 16

4.4 Comparing angles and constructing equal angles (1)

Learning objective

Construct and reason about angles

A. Multiple choice questions

1. A 10 degree angle viewed under a $100\times$ magnifier is (   ).

   A. $0.1°$　　　　 B. $1°$　　　　 C. $10°$　　　　 D. $1000°$

2. Take any point P inside $\angle AOB$ and draw line OP. Then there must be (   ).

   A. $\angle AOB > \angle AOP$　　　　 B. $\angle AOP = \angle BOP$

   C. $\angle AOP > \angle BOP$　　　　 D. $\angle BOP > \angle AOP$

3. At 8 o'clock, the angle between the hour hand and the minute hand on a clock is (   ).

   A. an acute angle　　　　 B. a right angle

   C. an obtuse angle　　　　 D. a straight angle

B. Fill in the blanks

4. Look at the diagram and compare the angles.

   Method 1 (by measuring): Use a _____ to measure the degrees of the two angles and then compare.

   Method 2 (by overlapping): Move $\angle FED$ so point _____ coincides with point _____, side ED and side BC _____ with each other, and EF and BA are on the _____.

   If EF is _____, then $\angle FED < \angle ABC$

   if EF is _____, then $\angle FED = \angle ABC$

   if EF is _____, then $\angle FED > \angle ABC$.

Diagram for question 4

5 When comparing two angles, there are three possible results. One angle can be _____, or _____, or _____ the other angle.

6 As shown in the diagram, $\angle BAM = \angle CAM$. If $\angle BAM$ is flipped over along AM, side AB and side AC will be _____. If AB is equal to AC, then point B and point C will be _____.

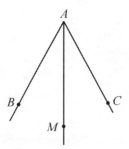

Diagram for question 6

7 In the diagram, $\alpha > \beta$. If β is flipped over along AD, side AC will be in the _____ area α.

(Choose 'interior' or 'exterior' to fill in.)

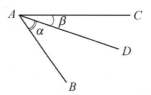

Diagram for question 7

 ## C. Questions that require solutions

8 The diagram shows an angle marked α. Use a ruler and compasses to draw $\angle AOB = \alpha$.

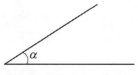

Diagram for question 8

9 Use a protractor to draw an angle $AOB = 80°$, and then in the interior area of $\angle AOB$, draw an angle $BOC = 50°$.

10 The diagram shows OA, OB, OC and OD, representing the directions of east, south, west and north, all starting from O.

Draw points E, F, G and H as indicated:

(a) Point E is 2 cm due north of point O.

(b) Point F is 3 cm in the direction 60° east of north from O.

(c) Point G is 1.5 cm southeast of point O.

(d) Point H is 2 cm in the direction 40° west of south from O.

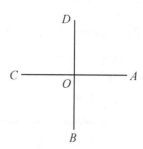

Diagram for question 10

11 As shown in the diagram, 3 lines from O are drawn and all are inside $\angle AOE$. How many angles are there in the diagram? What if 4 lines were drawn? How about 5 lines? If n ($n > 1$) lines are drawn from O, how many angles will there be in the diagram?

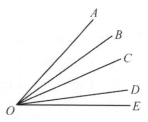

Diagram for question 11

4.5 Comparing angles and constructing equal angles (2)

Learning objective

Construct and reason about angles

A. Multiple choice questions

1. Given $\angle AOB = 93°$ and $\angle COD$ is a right angle, then we have (   ).

    A. $\angle AOB > \angle COD$

    B. $\angle AOB < \angle COD$

    C. $\angle AOB = \angle COD$

    D. none of the above

2. Among the following statements, the incorrect one is (   ).

    A. The size of an angle is not related to the lengths of its sides.

    B. The size of an angle is measured in degrees.

    C. On a clock face, the angle formed by the hour hand and the minute hand at 5 o'clock is equal to the angle formed by the hour hand and the minute hand at 7 o'clock.

    D. There are no equal angles among the four angles formed by two intersecting lines.

3. To describe the direction of a building from a point, the standard maths language is (   ).

    A. 110° west of north

    B. 70° west of south

    C. 160° south of east

    D. 70° south of west

4. Among the following statements about a triangle, the correct one is (   ).

    A. There are at least two acute angles.

    B. There are at least two right angles.

    C. There are at least two obtuse angles.

    D. None of the above is correct.

B. Fill in the blanks

5 Look at the diagram below. Construct an angle on the right so that it is equal to the angle given on the left. Fill in the blanks.

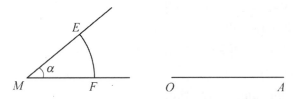

Diagram for question 5

Given an angle α, use a ruler and compasses to draw $\angle AOB$, so that $\angle AOB = \alpha$.

Solution:

(1) Draw OA.

(2) Use the vertex of angle α as the centre and a as the radius of a circle to draw an arc, intersecting the two sides of angle α at E and F respectively.

(3) Use _____ as the centre and _____ as the radius of a circle to draw an arc, intersecting OA at the point C.

(4) Use _____ as the centre and _____ as the radius of a circle to draw an arc, intersecting the previous arc at point D.

(5) Passing through D, draw OB. $\angle AOB$ is the angle required to draw.

6 As shown in the diagram, points A, O and B are on the same line, $\angle COD = 45°$ and $\angle BOD = 90°$. If $\angle BOD$ is turned $135°$ clockwise around O, then three points _____ are on the same line.

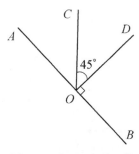

Diagram for question 6

7 Draw the diagram with the given conditions: $\angle AOB = 170°$, $\angle AOC = 70°$ and $\angle BOD = 60°$. Then there are _____ different values of the degrees of $\angle COD$ (less than $180°$).

C. Questions that require solutions

8 Use a protractor to measure the angles in the diagram and then answer the questions.

   (a) How many acute angles are equal to each other?

   What are the degrees?

   (b) How many obtuse angles are equal to each other?

   What are the degrees?

   (c) How many right angles are there?

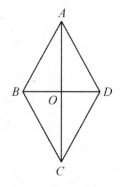

Diagram for question 8

9 Given $\angle A = (3x + 70)°$, $\angle B = (7x - 50)°$ and $\angle A = \angle B$, find the degrees of $\angle A$ and $\angle B$.

10 In the diagram, point A represents City A and point D represents City D.

(a) If City B is $60°$ west of south from City A, draw the line from City A to City B.

(b) If City C is $30°$ east of north from City A and $60°$ east of north from City D, locate the position of City C (denoted by point C).

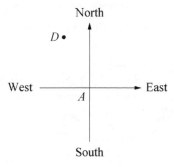

Diagram for question 10

11 Given $\angle AOB = 40°$, draw OC inside the angle from point O to make $\angle AOC$: $\angle COB = 2 : 3$. Find the degree of the angle between OC and the bisector of $\angle AOB$. (Note: The **bisector** of an angle divides the angle into two equal halves.)

4.6 Constructing sums, differences and multiples of angles (1)

Learning objective

Construct and reason about angles

A. Multiple choice questions

1. When a clock face shows $9:30$, the angle between the minute hand and the hour hand is (   ).
   A. $75°$ B. $105°$ C. $90°$ D. $135°$

2. If α and β are acute angles, then $\alpha + \beta$ satisfies (   ).
   A. $0° < \alpha + \beta < 90°$ B. $0° < \alpha + \beta < 180°$
   C. $\alpha + \beta = 180°$ D. $90° < \alpha + \beta < 180°$

3. The angle below that cannot be drawn using a set square is (   ).
   A. $15°$ B. $75°$ C. $65°$ D. $135°$

4. As shown in the diagram, $\angle AOC = \angle BOD = 78°$ and $\angle BOC = 35°$, then $\angle AOD$ is equal to (   ).
   A. $86°$ B. $121°$
   C. $156°$ D. $113°$

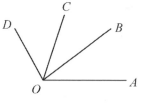

Diagram for question 4

B. Fill in the blanks

5. As shown in the diagram, $\angle AOD = $ _____ $+ \angle AOB$, $\angle COD = $ _____ $- \angle BOC$, $\angle AOC = $ _____ $+$ _____ $= $ _____ $- \angle COD$.

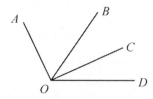

Diagram for question 5

112

6 As shown in the diagram, $\angle AOC = \angle BOD = 90°$ and $\angle AOB = 68°$, then $\angle COD = $ _____ .

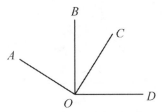

Diagram for question 6

7 As shown in the diagram, lines AB and CD intersect at point O and $\angle AOE = 90°$. If $\angle DOB = 128°$, then $\angle DOE = $ _____ , and $\angle AOD = $ _____ .

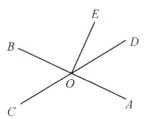

Diagram for question 7

8 If the ratio of two angles is $2 : 5$ and the difference is $30°$, then the two angles are _____ ° and _____ °.

9 As shown in the diagram, OA, OB, OC and OD have the same endpoint O. In $\angle AOB$, $\angle BOC$, $\angle COD$ and $\angle AOD$, there are at most _____ acute angles.

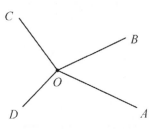

Diagram for question 9

10 As shown in the diagram, $\angle ABC =$ _____ + _____ ,
$\angle ADC - \angle ADB =$ _____ , $\angle BDE +$ _____ $= \angle BDC$.

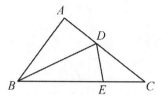

Diagram for question 10

11 As shown in the diagram, $AOE = 110°$, $\angle AOB = 30°$, $\angle BOC = 32°$ and OC bisects $\angle BOD$; then $\angle COE =$ _____ , $\angle AOD =$ _____ and $\angle BOE =$ _____ .

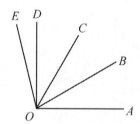

Diagram for question 11

12 Given $\alpha = 110°$, and $\beta = 20°$, then $2\beta =$ _____ and $\frac{1}{2}(\alpha + \beta) =$ _____ .

C. Questions that require solutions

13 Given $\alpha + \beta = 90°$, $\alpha = (7x - 2)°$ and $\beta = (3x + 2)°$, find α and β.

14 Given $\alpha = \angle ABC$, $\beta = \angle DEF$, use a protractor to draw the following angles.
(a) $\gamma = \alpha + \beta$ (b) $\delta = \alpha + 2\beta$
(c) $\theta = 2\alpha - \beta$ (d) $\varphi = 3\beta$

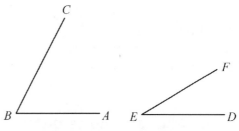

Diagram for question 14

15 The diagram shows three lines AB, CD and EF with a common point O, and $\angle BOC = 90°$. If $\angle AOF = \beta$, then how would you represent $\angle EOC$?

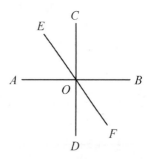

Diagram for question 15

16 First use a protractor to draw $\angle AOB = 70°$ and then draw a line to make $\angle AOC = 80$. What is the degree of $\angle BOC$?

17 What is the angle that the hour hand has turned through from $3:45$ p.m. to $8:21$ p.m.?

4.7 Constructing sums, differences and multiples of angles (2)

Learning objective

Construct and reason about angles

A. Multiple choice questions

1 As shown in the diagram, lines AB and CD intersect at point O, OA bisects $\angle EOC$ and $\angle EOC = 72°$; then the degree of $\angle BOD$ is (   ).

A. $30°$ B. $36°$ C. $20°$ D. $40°$

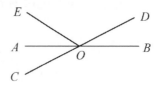

Diagram for question 1

2 As shown in the diagram, OC is the bisector of $\angle AOB$, OD bisects $\angle AOC$ and $\angle COD = 15°$; then $\angle AOB = ($ $)$.

A. $15°$ B. $30°$ C. $45°$ D. $60°$

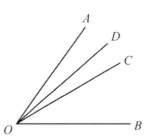

Diagram for question 2

3 As shown in the diagram, $\angle AOC = 90°$, $\angle COB = \alpha$ and OD bisects $\angle AOB$; then $\angle COD = ($ $)$.

A. $\dfrac{\alpha}{2}$ B. $45° - \dfrac{\alpha}{2}$ C. $45° - \alpha$ D. $90° - \alpha$

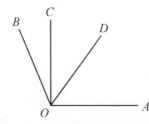

Diagram for question 3

B. Fill in the blanks

4 As shown in the diagram, $\angle AOB = \angle AOC$ and $\angle BOC = 86°$; then $\angle AOB =$ _____ degrees.

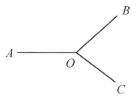

Diagram for question 4

5 As shown in the diagram, $\angle AOC = \angle BOD$ and $\angle BOC = 2\angle AOB$; then $\angle BOD =$ _____ $\angle COD$.

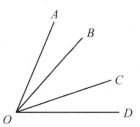

Diagram for question 5

6 As shown in the diagram, OB is the bisector of $\angle AOC$ and OD is the bisector of $\angle COE$. If $\angle AOE = 128°$, then $\angle BOD =$ _____.

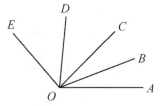

Diagram for question 6

7 As shown in the diagram, if $\angle AEC = 60°$ and ED bisects $\angle AEC$, then $\angle AED =$ _____ $\angle BEC$.

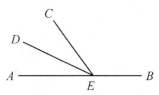

Diagram for question 7

8 Cut out an angle of 120° and fold it twice. The angle is _____ degrees. If you fold it three times, the angle is _____ degrees. If you cut an angle of $n°$ and fold it _____ times, then it is an angle of $\frac{1}{32}n°$.

9 As shown in the diagram, OC bisects $\angle AOB$ and $\angle AOC = 32°$; then $\angle AOB =$ _____ and $\angle BOC =$ _____.

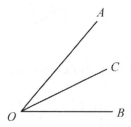

Diagram for question 9

10 There are two set squares, one with $90-45-45$ degree angles and the other with $30-60-90$ degree angles. The number of angles greater than 0° but less than 180° that can be drawn using these two set squares is _____.

11 As shown in the diagram, points A, B and C are on the same line. Given $\angle ABD = 3x°$, $\angle DBE = (30+x)°$ and $\angle CBE = (3x+10)°$, then $x =$ _____.

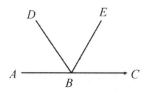

Diagram for question 11

12 As shown in the diagram, $\angle BOC : \angle AOD = 2 : 3$, $\angle AOB : \angle COD = 5 : 2$ and $\angle AOB$ is 10° less than the sum of the other three angles, then $\angle AOB =$ _____, $\angle BOC =$ _____, $\angle COD =$ _____ and $\angle AOD =$ _____.

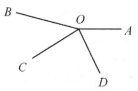

Diagram for question 12

C. Questions that require solutions

13 As shown in the diagram, given $\angle AOD = 81°$, OC bisects $\angle BOD$, $\angle AOB = (x + 8)°$ and $\angle COD = (3x - 2)°$, find the degrees of $\angle AOB$ and $\angle COD$.

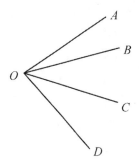

Diagram for question 13

14 As shown in the diagram, lines AB and CD intersect at point O, $OE \perp AB$, OF bisects $\angle AOC$, and $\angle DOE = 18°$. Find the degree of $\angle COF$. (Note: The symbol '$\perp$' means 'is perpendicular to'.)

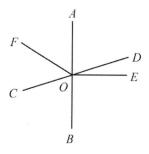

Diagram for question 14

15 Given that the sum of the three angles of any triangle is $180°$; as shown in the diagram, in triangle ABC, BO and CO bisect $\angle ABC$ and $\angle ACB$ respectively. If $\angle A = 56°$, find the degree of $\angle BOC$.

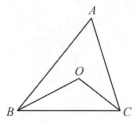

Diagram for question 15

16 As shown in the diagram, OD bisects $\angle BOC$, OE and OF divide $\angle AOC$ into three equal parts.

(a) If $\angle BOF = 100°$, find the degree of $\angle DOE$.

(b) If $\angle BOF = 100°$ and $\angle COD = 35°$, find the degree of $\angle AOF$.

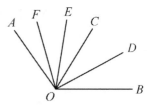

Diagram for question 16

4.8 Complementary angles and supplementary angles

 Learning objective

Use properties of complementary and supplementary angles to solve related problems

 A. Multiple choice questions

1 If angle $\alpha = n°$, and α has both a complementary angle and a supplementary angle, then the range of n is (   ).

A. $90 < n < 180$ B. $0 < n < 90$

C. $n = 90$ D. $n = 180$

2 As shown in the diagram, John walked 50 m from point A to point B in the direction of $70°$ east of north. Mary walked 80 m from point A to point C in the direction $15°$ west of south. Then $\angle BAC = ($ $)$.

A. $85°$ B. $160°$

C. $125°$ D. $105°$

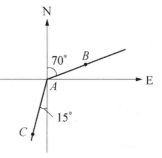

Diagram for question 2

 Among the following statements, the correct one is (   ).

A. The complementary angle of an acute angle is an acute angle.

B. The supplementary angle of an acute angle is an acute angle.

C. The complementary angle of an obtuse angle is an obtuse angle.

D. The supplementary angle of an obtuse angle is an obtuse angle.

4 If the ratio of an acute angle and its complementary angle is $5 : 4$, then the supplementary angle of the acute angle is (   ).

A. $100°$ B. $120°$ C. $130°$ D. $140°$

 B. Fill in the blanks

5 If an angle is equal to its complementary angle, then the angle is _____°. If an angle is equal to its supplementary angle, then the angle is _____°.

6 The supplementary angle of an angle is _____° greater than its complementary angle.

7 If an angle is twice its complementary angle, then the angle is _____°. If it is twice its supplementary angle, then the angle is _____°.

8 If the complementary angle of an angle and its supplementary angle supplement each other, then the angle is _____°.

9 Given $\alpha = 20°$, $\beta = 30°$, $\gamma = 60°$ and $\delta = 150°$, then angle β is the complementary angle of _____ and _____ is the supplementary angle of angle δ.

10 If $\alpha = 39°$, then the complementary angle β of $\alpha =$ _____, the supplementary angle γ of $\alpha =$ _____. $\gamma - \beta =$ _____.

11 If $\alpha + \beta = 90°$, $\gamma + \beta = 90°$ and $\alpha = 40°$, then $\gamma =$ _____. The result is based on the fact that the complementary angles of the same angle are _____.

12 If $\alpha = 130°$ and $\beta = 10°$, then the supplementary angle of $\frac{1}{2}(\alpha + \beta)$ is _____.

13 If $\alpha = 70°$ and $\beta = 30°$, then the complementary angle of $\frac{1}{5}(\alpha - \beta)$ is _____.

14 From 2 : 35 to 4 : 15, the minute hand turns _____ degrees and the hour hand turns _____ degrees.

C. Questions that require solutions

15 The supplementary angle of an angle is $18°$ greater than twice its complementary angle. Find the angle.

16 The ratio of the supplementary angle of an angle to its complementary angle is $31 : 13$. Find the angle.

17 As shown in the diagram, point O is on the line MN, OP bisects $\angle MOQ$ and OH bisects $\angle NOQ$. Write the complementary and supplementary angles of $\angle POM$.

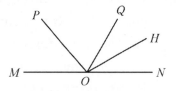

Diagram for question 17

18 Given x and y are positive integers, the degree of angle α is $(3x+5)°$, the degree of angle β is $(3y-2)°$ and α and β supplement each other, find the sum of all possible values of x and y.

4.9   Circle and its circumference

Learning objective

Calculate and solve problems involving circumferences of circles; use related terms

A. Multiple choice questions

1 Among the following statements about a circle, the incorrect one is (   ).

   A. The circumference is the length of the edge around a circle.

   B. The diameter of a circle is twice its radius.

   C. The ratio of the circumference of a circle to its diameter is always the same no matter what the size of the circle is.

   D. π is the ratio of the circumference of a circle to its radius.

> π is the ratio of the circumference of a circle to its diameter. It is an infinite non-repeating decimal and is approximately 3.141 593. (Note: unless otherwise indicated, we take π as 3.14 in this book.)

2 Andy drew a circle with radius 2 cm. Max used a string with length 4π cm to form a circle. The correct statement of the following is (   ).

   A. Andy's circle is larger. ,

   B. Max's circle is larger.

   C. The two circles are of the same size.

   D. The sizes of the two circles cannot be compared.

3 To draw a circle whose circumference is 28.26 cm, the distance between the two legs of a compass on a ruler should be about (   ).

   A. 9 cm   B. 3 cm   C. 4.5 cm   D. 1.5 cm

4 As shown in the diagram, if we compare the circumference of the outer circle with the sum of the circumferences of the two inner circles, then the result is (   ).

   A. They are of the same length.

   B. The circumference of the outer circle is longer.

   C. The sum of the circumference of the inner circles is longer.

   D. uncertain

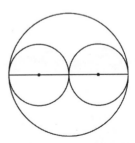

Diagram for question 4

B. Fill in the blanks

5 If the radius of a circle is r, then the circumference of the circle is _____ .
Given the diameter of a circle is 4 cm, its circumference is _____ cm.

6 The length of the hour hand of a clock is 10 cm. The hour hand runs _____ cm
for 12 hours.

7 There is a semicircle-shaped window with diameter 1 m. The perimeter of this
semicircle shape is _____ m.

8 If the diameter of a circle is increased to five times the original length, then its
circumference is increased to _____ times the original length.

9 If the radius of a circle is increased by 3 cm, then its circumference is increased
by _____ cm.

C. Questions that require solutions

10 Fill in the table.

Radius r	Diameter d	Circumference C
5		
	18	
		69.08

11 The diagram shows a circular road. The circumference of the outer circle is 62.8 m and
that of the inner circle is 50.24 m. Find the width of the road.

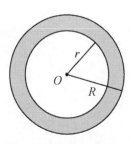

Diagram for question 11

12 In the diagram, AB is the diameter of the outer circle and has a length of 20 cm. The radius of the inner circle is 6 cm. Find the perimeter of the shaded part.

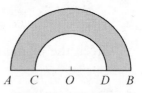

A   C   O   D   B

Diagram for question 12

13 A copper wire is used up completely after winding around a circular pipe 12 times. The diameter of the pipe is 30 cm. What is the approximate length of the copper wire?

14 The outer diameter of each tyre on Will's bike is 50 cm. If the tyres rotate 300 times per minute on average, and Will's home is 4710 m away from the school, how long does it take him to go back home to pick up a book and then return to school immediately? (Note: Ignore the time spent at home getting the book.)

4.10 The area of a circle (1)

Learning objective

Calculate and solve problems involving areas of circles; use related terms

A. Multiple choice questions

1 If the length of the diameter of a circle is doubled, then its area is increased to ( ) times the original area.

A. 2 times   B. 4 times

C. 8 times   D. 16 times

2 If the circumference of a bigger circle is 4 times that of a smaller circle, then the area of the smaller circle is ( ) of the area of the bigger circle.

A. $\frac{1}{4}$ B. $\frac{1}{5}$ C. $\frac{1}{16}$ D. $\frac{1}{25}$

3 As shown in the diagram, the area of the circle is ( ) of the area of the semicircle.

A. $\frac{1}{3}$ B. $\frac{1}{2}$

C. $\frac{2}{3}$ D. $\frac{3}{4}$

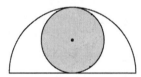

Diagram for question 3

B. Fill in the blanks

4 If the radius of a circle is r, then the area of the circle is _____. Given the diameter of a circle is 2 cm, its area is _____ cm².

5 A rectangular piece of paper has a length of 5 cm and a width of 4 cm. Cut out the largest possible circle from the paper. The area of the circle is _____ cm².

6 If the area of a circle is 153.86 cm², then the diameter of the circle is _____ cm.

7 If the circumference of a circle is 12.56 cm, then its area is _____ cm².

8 If the diameter of a smaller circle is equal to the radius of a bigger circle, then the area of the smaller circle is _____ of the area of the bigger circle. (Fill in with a fraction.)

9 If the radius of a circle is increased from 3 cm to 4 cm, then its area is increased by _____ cm².

C. Questions that require solutions

10 The diagram shows a semicircle. The diameter is 16 cm. What are its perimeter and area?

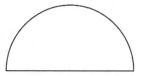

Diagram for question 10

11 The area of a circle is 5024 cm². What is its circumference?

12 A circle with diameter 12 cm was divided equally into 64 parts. Put these parts together to form approximately a rectangular shape. What is the length of the rectangle? What is its area?
(Hint: Refer to the diagram which shows part of the shape formed; drawing not to scale.)

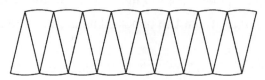

Diagram for question 12

13 Look at the diagram carefully. It shows three circle-based shapes and the shaded parts represent three punctuation marks: full stop, comma and question mark. They are to be used on a sign along a motorway. Given that the radius of each outer circle is R, the radius of each inner circle is r and $R = 2r$, if these shaded parts are to be evenly painted for use on the sign, which punctuation mark will use the most paint?

Diagram for question 13

14 The difference between the circumferences of two circles is 94.2 cm. Given that the radius of the bigger circle is twice the diameter of the smaller circle, find the sum of the areas of the two circles.

4.11   The area of a circle (2)

Learning objective

Calculate and solve problems involving areas of circles and composite shapes

A. Multiple choice questions

1. To draw a circle with an area of $28.26\,\text{cm}^2$, the measure of distance between the two legs of a compass should be (   ).

   A. 9 cm

   B. 3 cm

   C. 4.5 cm

   D. 1.5 cm

2. The area of a rectangle is $20\,\text{cm}^2$ and one of its sides is 5 cm. The area of the largest possible circle inside the rectangle is (   ).

   A. $4\pi\,\text{cm}^2$

   B. $5\pi\,\text{cm}^2$

   C. $8\pi\,\text{cm}^2$

   D. $10\pi\,\text{cm}^2$

3. If the circumference of a circle is increased to a times its original circumference, then its area is increased to (   ) times the original area.

   A. a B. $2a$ C. $4a$ D. a^2

B. Fill in the blanks

4. Fill in the table.

Radius r	Diameter d	Circumference C	Area of circle S
3 mm			
		15.7 cm	
	200 cm		
			200.96 m^2

5. There are two circles whose diameters are 4 cm and 6 cm. The area of the smaller circle is _____ of the area of the bigger circle. (Fill in with a fraction.)

6 If the radius of a circle is increased to 3 times the original radius, then its circumference is increased to _____ times the original circumference and its area is increased to _____ times the original area.

7 The perimeter of a semicircular garden is 5.14 m. The radius of the garden is _____ m, the area is _____ m^2.

C. Questions that require solutions

8 The diagram shows a circle-based shape, $AB = BC = CD = 3$ cm. Find the area of the shaded part.

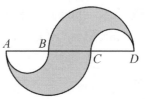

Diagram for question 8

9 The diagram shows two circles with the same centre. The diameter of the outer circle is 10 cm and the radius of the inner circle is 3 cm. What is the area of the shaded region?

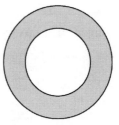

Diagram for question 9

10 The circumference of a circular fish pond is 100.48 m. There is a circular island with a radius of 6 m within the fish pond. Find the area of the water surface of the pond.

11 A rectangular flowerbed is 8 m long and 6 m wide. A smaller circular flowerbed was put in it to grow peonies so that the circular flowerbed had the largest possible area. Outside the circular part, the land is used for growing jasmines. What are the growing areas for peonies and jasmines?

12 The diagram shows a smaller square inside a bigger square. The largest possible circle is cut out from the smaller square. Find the area of the shaded part.

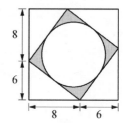

Diagram for question 12

13 The area of a circle is half of the area of a semicircle. The circumference of the circle is 18.84 cm. What is the perimeter of the semicircle?

Unit test 4

A. Multiple choice questions

1 Look at the diagram. The number of line segments in the figure is (   ).

A. 4

B. 5

C. 6

D. 7

Diagram for question 1

2 Among the following statements, (   ) of them is/are correct.

a. An angle that only has a supplementary angle but no complementary angle is an obtuse angle.

b. An acute angle has not only a complementary angle but also a supplementary angle.

c. The complementary angle of an acute angle is 90° less than its supplementary angle.

d. Of two supplementary angles, one must be an acute angle and the other an obtuse angle.

A. 4   B. 3   C. 2   D. 1

3 The diagram shows $\triangle ABC$, $\angle ACB = 2n°$, CD bisects the supplementary angle of $\angle ACB$; then $\angle ACD = $ (   ).

A. $180° - 2n°$ B. $90° - 2n°$

C. $90° - n°$ D. $180° - n°$

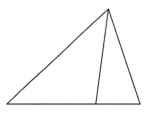

Diagram for question 3

4 Divide a straight angle into three equal parts. The angle formed by the bisectors of the two non-adjacent angles is (   ). [Hint: Draw a diagram to help answer the question.]

A. 90°   B. 120°   C. 135°   D. 150°

5 If the diameter of a circle is equal to the side length of a square, then comparing their areas, the result is (   ).

A. The area of the square is larger.   B. The area of the circle is larger.

C. Their areas are the same.   D. They cannot be compared.

6 There are two circles of different sizes. If the radius of the bigger circle is 3 times that of the smaller circle, then the circumference of the bigger circle is (   ) times that of the smaller circle.

A. 6   B. π C. 9   D. 3

7 In the diagram below, the number of figures that have the same perimeter of the shaded part is (   ).

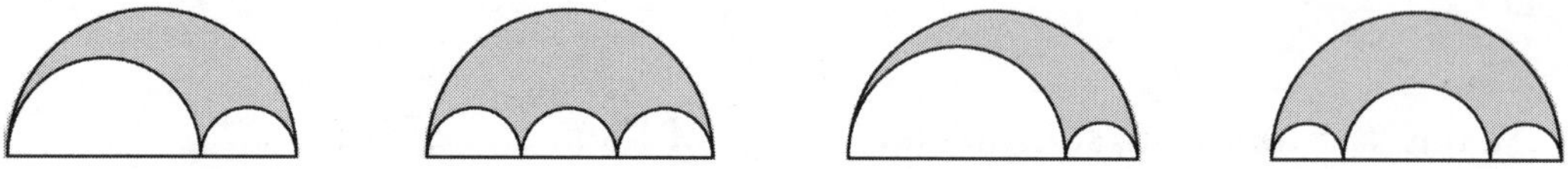

Diagram for question 7

A. 0   B. 2   C. 3   D. 4

B. Fill in the blanks

8 Among all the routes connecting two points, the _____ is the shortest.

9 Given that the radius of a semicircle is r, then the perimeter is _____.

10 The diagram shows three points A, B and C on the same line. There are _____ line segments.

Diagram for question 10

11 If point C is on the extension of line segment AB beyond A, then AC _____ BC. (Fill in with $<$ or $>$.)

12 As shown in the diagram, D is the midpoint of BC and $AC = 2$. If $AB = 10$, then $CD =$ _____.

Diagram for question 12

13 As shown in the diagram, O is a point on line AD, $\angle AOB = 45°$ and OC bisects $\angle BOD$; then $\angle COD = $ _____ degrees.

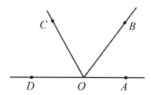

Diagram for question 13

14 If the difference of two supplementary angles is $22°$, then the two angles are _____ degrees and _____ degrees respectively.

15 Calculate: $180° - 62° = $ _____.

16 Given that the circumference of a circular flowerbed is 9.42 m, a circular fence is built 1 m outside the edge of the flowerbed, then the shortest length of the fence is _____ m.

17 Given two angle α and β, $\alpha = (x + 10)°$, $\beta = (x - 30)°$, and α and β complement each other, then $\alpha = $ _____ degrees.

18 As shown in the diagram, $\angle AOB = 72°$, OC bisects $\angle AOB$, $OD \perp OC$, then $\angle AOD = $ _____ degrees.

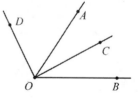

19 On a clock face, the angle that the hour hand turns in an hour is _____.

Diagram for question 18

20 The complementary angle of an angle is equal to the angle itself. The angle equals _____.

21 Starting from O, OA is in the direction $25°$ east of north and OB is in the direction $70°$ east of south. $\angle AOB = $ _____ degrees.

22 Given point B is on line AC, segment $AB = 8$ cm, $AC = 18$ cm, and P and Q are the midpoints of AB and AC respectively, then the length of segment PQ is _____.

23 Using a set square, we can directly draw angles of $30°$, $45°$, $60°$ and $90°$, and through sums and difference of angles we can also draw some special angles such as $75°$, $120°$, $135°$ and $165°$. The other angles less than a straight angle that we can draw using a set square are _____ .

24 If the circumference of a circle is 37.68 cm, then its area is _____ cm^2.

25 There are two circles. If the radius of the bigger circle is twice that of the smaller circle, then the circumference of the smaller circle is _____ of that of the bigger circle, and the area of the smaller circle is _____ of that of the bigger circle. (Fill in each blank with a fraction.)

C. Questions that require solutions

26 The diagram shows two line segments a and b. Construct a line segment that is equal to $2a - b$. (You don't need to write the steps, but show your drawing.)

a b

Diagram for question 26

27 The diagram shows two angles $α$ and $β$. Construct: $\angle AOB = α + 2β$. (You don't need to write the steps, but show your drawing.)

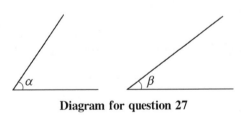

Diagram for question 27

28 The supplementary angle of an angle is $10°$ greater than 3 times the complementary angle of the angle. Find the angle.

29 Ruler and compass construction: Construct the midpoint M of segment AB and the midpoint N of segment BC. (You don't need to write the steps, but show your drawing.)

30 As shown in the diagram, $AB = BC = CD$ and the sum of all the segments in the diagram is 18 cm. Find the length of AB.

A B C D

Diagram for question 30

31 A clock face shows that the time has moved from $15:05$ to $15:10$ on a day. Accordingly, how many degrees has the minute hand turned? How many degrees has the hour hand turned?

32 Find the perimeter of the shaded part in the diagram. (unit: cm)

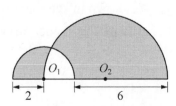

Diagram for question 32

33 Given that the difference between the areas of two circles is 209 cm^2, the circumference of the larger circle is $1\frac{1}{9}$ times that of the smaller circle, find the area of each circle.

34 As shown in the diagram, lines AB and CD intersect at point O, $OE \perp AB$ at point O and $\angle DOE = 50°$. Find $\angle BOC$.

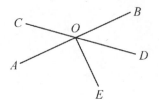

Diagram for question 34

35 Extend segment AB beyond B to D so that $DB = \frac{3}{2}AB$. Extend BA beyond A to point C so that $CA = AB$. How many times AB is CD ? What fraction of CD is BC?

36 As shown in the diagram, given that the side length of the square is 4 cm, find the area of the shaded area.

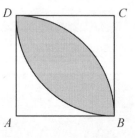

Diagram for question 36

Chapter 5　Transformation of figures

5.1　Translation

 Learning objective

Identify and reason about translation of figures; draw images after a translation

 A. Multiple choice questions

1 Among the following four figures, (　　) of them can each be viewed as being the result of a translation.

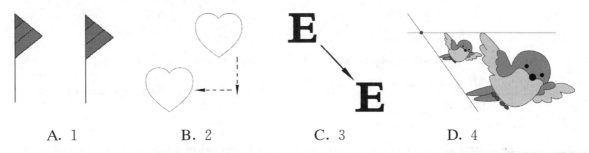

　A. 1　　　　　　B. 2　　　　　　C. 3　　　　　　D. 4

2 The diagram shows rectangle $A'B'C'D'$ which is obtained by a translation of rectangle $ABCD$. Among the following statements, the incorrect one is (　　).

A. Translating rectangle $ABCD$ 4 units up and 9 units right gives rectangle $A'B'C'D'$.

B. Translating rectangle $ABCD$ 9 units right and 4 units up gives rectangle $A'B'C'D'$.

C. Translating rectangle $ABCD$ in the direction of BD' by the distance of the length of segment BD' gives rectangle $A'B'C'D'$.

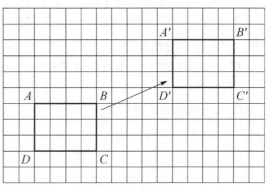

Diagram for question 2

D. Translating rectangle $ABCD$ in the direction of BB' by the distance of the length of segment BB' gives rectangle $A'B'C'D'$.

B. Fill in the blanks

3 Under a translation, every point of the figure (object) must move the _____ distance in the _____ direction, and the obtained figure (image) has the same shape and _____ as the original figure.

4 In $\triangle ABC$, $AB = 5$ cm and $\angle C = 90°$. After a translation, it coincides with $\triangle A'B'C'$ with the images of points A, B and C being points A', B' and C', then $A'B' = $ _____ cm, $\angle C' = $ _____ .

5 If segment $MN = 6$ cm and point P is the midpoint of MN, then segment PN can be viewed as the result of translating MP by a distance of _____ in the direction of _____ . (Hint: You may draw a diagram to help you answer.)

6 In the diagram, segment $A'B'$ is obtained by a translation of segment AB, $AB = 4$ cm and $AA' = 5$ cm, then segment AB is translated by a distance of _____ in the direction of _____ .

$A \overline{\hspace{2cm}} B$

$A' \overline{\hspace{2cm}} B'$

Diagram for question 6

7 If quadrilateral $A_1B_1C_1D_1$ is obtained from a translation of quadrilateral $ABCD$ by moving 3 units up, and D_1 is the image of D, then segment $DD_1 = $ _____ .

C. Questions that require solutions

8 The diagram shows a pentagon $ABCDE$ on 2-cm square grid paper. Translate the pentagon so that point A moves to point A'. Label the image $\triangle A'B'C'E'F'$ and describe the translation with the moving directions and distances (in cm).

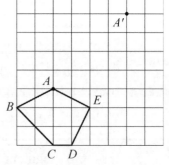

Diagram for question 8

9 The diagram shows half of a circle on a 1-cm square grid paper. Translate it so that point O coincides with point O' after translation.

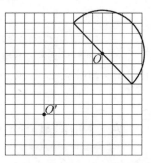

Diagram for question 9

10 (a) Draw the image of $\triangle ABC$ under the translation in the direction of AD for a distance of 2 cm.

(b) Take any point P in segment AB, and draw the image of P under the above translation.

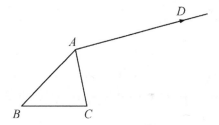

Diagram for question 10

5.2 Rotation

Identify and reason about the rotations of figures; draw images after a rotation

 A. Multiple choice questions

1 In the following four diagrams, the one in which $\triangle A'B'C'$ cannot be obtained by rotating $\triangle ABC$ is (   ).

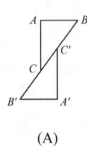

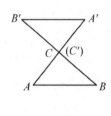

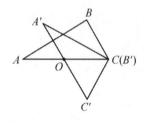

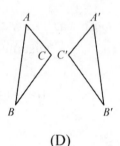

(A)	(B)	(C)	(D)

2 In the following, the number of figures that are each identical to their starting position after a rotation of $90°$ is (   ).

A. 4   B. 3   C. 2   D. 1

3 Among the following statements about rotation and translation, the correct one is (   ).

A. A rotation changes the shape of a figure.

B. The figure obtained from rotation of a figure can be also obtained through a translation of the figure.

C. A point and its image of a rotation have equal distance from the centre of rotation.

D. Both translation and rotation can change the position and the size of the figure.

4 As shown in the diagram, rotating the right-angled triangle ABC (where $\angle ABC = 60°$) around point B for a certain degree clockwise gives triangle $A'B'C'$, and points A, B and C' are on the same line. Then the angle of rotation is (   ).

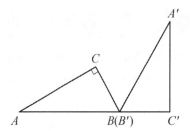

A. $30°$ B. $60°$

C. $90°$ D. $120°$

Diagram for question 4

5 As shown in the diagram, after a rotation anticlockwise, $\triangle ABC$ coincides with $\triangle ADE$, and $\angle BAE = 60°$. The centre of rotation is _____ , the image of point C is _____ , and the angle of rotation is _____ .

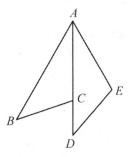

Diagram for question 5

6 The diagram shows a triangle ABC, $AB = AC$, $\angle BAC = 100°$ and D is a point on BC. If after a rotation, $\triangle ABD$ moves to the position of $\triangle ACE$, then the centre of rotation is _____ , the image angle of $\angle BAD$ is _____ , the image segment of AD is _____ , and $\angle DAE = $ _____ °.

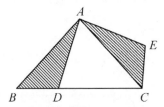

Diagram for question 6

B. Fill in the blanks

7 The diagram shows a right-angled isosceles triangle △*ABC*, ∠*BAC* = 90°. If after a rotation, △*AEC* coincides with △*AFB*, then point _____ is the centre of rotation and the angle of rotation is _____ or _____.

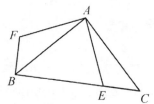

Diagram for question 7

8 As shown in the diagram, point *D* is within the equilateral triangle *ABC*. After a rotation, △*BDC* coincides with △*AEC*. △*DCE* is an _____ triangle. (Identify what type of triangle it is.)

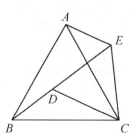

Diagram for question 8

9 As shown in the diagram, △*A′B′C′* is generated by rotating △*ABC* 80° anticlockwise about point *O*. The angle of rotation is _____, *BO* = _____, and ∠*COC′* = _____°.

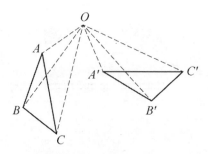

Diagram for question 9

C. Questions that require solutions

10 Given point E is a point on the side CD of square $ABCD$, draw the image triangle obtained by rotating $\triangle ADE$ 90° about point A clockwise. Indicate the image points and the angle of rotation.

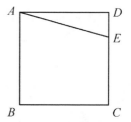

Diagram for question 10

11 In the 10×5 square grid, each small square has a side length of 1 unit. Translating $\triangle ABC$ 4 units right gives $\triangle A'B'C'$, and further rotating $\triangle A'B'C'$ about point A' 90° anticlockwise gives $\triangle A''B''C''$. Draw $\triangle A'B'C'$ and $\triangle A''B''C''$.

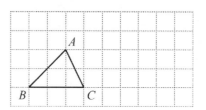

Diagram for question 11

12 On the diagram, draw the image of the figure after a rotation of 90° anticlockwise about point O.

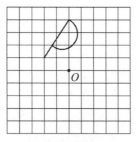

Diagram for question 12

13 As shown in the diagram, quadrilateral $ABCD$ is a square with side length 1 unit, $DE = \dfrac{1}{4}$, $AD = 1$, and $\triangle ABF$ is a rotation of $\triangle ADE$.

(a) The centre of the rotation is _____ .

(b) It is rotated _____ degrees.

(c) Connecting EF, what type of triangle is $\triangle AEF$?

(d) The area of $\triangle AEF$ is _____ .

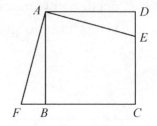

Diagram for question 13

5.3 Rotational symmetry

Learning objective

Identify and reason about rotational symmetry

A. Multiple choice questions

1. In the following figures, the one that can be viewed as a result of rotating a part of it around a point 180° is (　　).

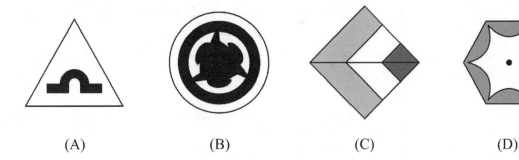

(A)   (B)   (C)   (D)

2. Given a line segment, a square, a circle, a rectangle, a parallelogram and an equilateral triangle, there are (　　) of them which have point symmetry①.
   A. 6   B. 5   C. 4   D. 3

B. Fill in the blanks

3. The range of the angle of rotation for a figure of rotational symmetry is _____ .

4. Point symmetry is _____ rotational symmetry; rotational symmetry is _____ point symmetry. (Choose 'definitely' or 'not definitely' to fill in.)

---

① Note: Point symmetry (also called central symmetry) is a special type of rotational symmetry in which the angle of rotation is 180°. For each point in a figure with point symmetry, there exists a matching point found directly opposite to it on the other side of the centre.

5 As shown in the diagram, if quadrilateral *CDEF* can be rotated to coincide with square *ABCD*, then the number of the points on the plane that can be the centre of rotation is _____ .

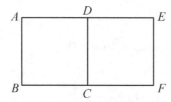

Diagram for question 5

6 The figure can be viewed as one obtained by rotating a rhombus with a diagonal _____ times, and each time it is rotated _____ degrees.

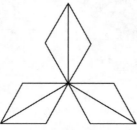

Diagram for question 6

7 Figure (1) can be rotated _____ degrees in a _____ direction to coincide with itself.

Figure (2) can be rotated _____ degrees in a _____ direction to coincide with itself.

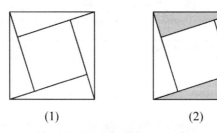

(1)   (2)

Diagram for question 7

C. Questions that require solutions

8 Look at the following figures carefully. Write the angle of rotation for each figure and indicate which figures have point symmetry.

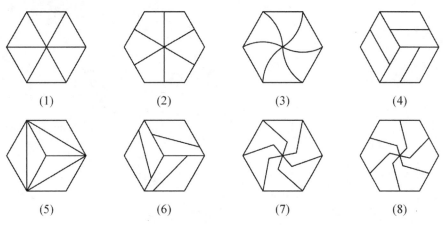

Diagram for question 8

9 The diagram shows part of a pattern for a square tablecloth. Use the coordinate grid given below to draw the figures obtained by rotating the figure clockwise $90°$, $180°$ and $270°$, respectively, and state what type of shape each figure obtained is.

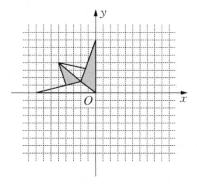

Diagram for question 9

10 The diagram shows a quadrilateral combining two equilateral triangles.

(a) Does the figure have rotational symmetry? Does it also have point symmetry? If so, identify the centre of rotation for point symmetry.

(b) If △*ACD* can be rotated to coincide with △*ABC*, then how many points on the plane could be the centre of rotation? Indicate all of the points.

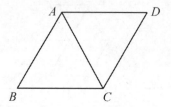

Diagram for question 10

5.4 Folding and figures with reflection symmetry

 Learning objective

Identify rotational and reflection symmetry in plane shapes

 A. Multiple choice questions

1 The following figure that has both reflection symmetry and rotational symmetry is ( ).

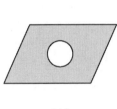   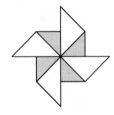   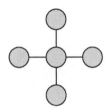   

(A)   (B)   (C)   (D)

2 The following figure that has both point symmetry and reflection symmetry is ( ).
A. an equilateral triangle   B. a parallelogram
C. a pentagon   D. a square

3 The diagram shows $\triangle ABC$, $\angle C = 90°$, and D is a point on AC. Fold $\triangle BCD$ along line BD so that point C coincides with point E on side AB. If $DC = 5$ cm, then ( ) of the following statement(s) is/are true.

(1) $ED = 5$ cm

(2) $ED = 4$ cm

(3) ED is perpendicular to AB.

(4) ED is not necessarily perpendicular to AB.

A. 1   B. 2   C. 3   D. 4

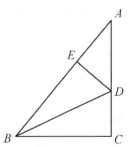

Diagram for question 3

 B. Fill in the blanks

4 If a figure is folded along a line and the two parts of the figure divided by the line coincide with each other, then the figure has _____ , and the line is called _____ .

5 In a figure with reflection symmetry, the corresponding segments are _____ , and the corresponding angles[1] are _____ .

6 Among a square, a parallelogram, a circle, an isosceles triangle, a segment and a rectangle, _____ does/do not have reflection symmetry.

7 If an equilateral triangle has n reflection lines, then $n =$ _____ .

 ## C. Questions that require solutions

8 Draw all the lines of symmetry on each figure below.

Diagram for question 8

9 Figure (1) below shows a square tile. Figures (2) and (3) show two new squares that are formed using four square tiles. Shade them to show how the tiles are exactly placed to form the new squares as shown in these two figures. (Each shaded figure must have line symmetry.)

  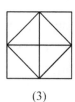

(1)　　　　　　　(2)　　　　　　　(3)

Diagram for question 9

――――――――――

[1] Two segments (or angles, etc.) are called corresponding segments (or angles, etc.) under a reflection if one is the image of the other under the reflection.

5.5　Reflection symmetry

Learning objective

Identify and reason about reflection symmetry

A. Multiple choice questions

1 A circle has (　　) line(s) of symmetry.

　　A. 0　　　　　　　　B. 1　　　　　　　　C. 2　　　　　　　　D. infinitely many

2 The following statement that is incorrect is (　　).

　　A. Reflection symmetry can refer to two figures, describing a relationship about them.

　　B. Reflection symmetry can refer to one figure, describing a special feature of the figure itself.

　　C. Two figures that are reflectively symmetric can fit exactly over each other.

　　D. Two figures that fit exactly over each other have reflection symmetry.

B. Fill in the blanks

3 If two figures are symmetric about a line, then the line segment joining a point and its image is _____ to and _____ by the symmetry line. If a segment joining two points is _____ to and _____ by a line, then the two points are symmetric about the line (also called the 'mirror line' or 'line of symmetry').

4 If two figures are symmetric about a line, and a line segment and its image (or their extensions) intersect in a point, then the point must lie on _____.

5 The diagram shows $\triangle ABC$ and its image $\triangle A'B'C'$ under reflection about line l. $\angle B = 75°$ and $A'C' = 15$. Then $\angle B' =$ _____ , $AC =$ _____ .

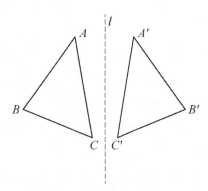

Diagram for question 5

153

C. Questions that require solutions

6 Draw the image of A when reflected in the line MN. Label this A′.

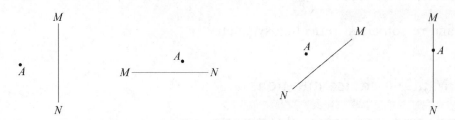

Diagram for question 6

7 Draw line segment A′B′ that is symmetric to line segment AB with respect to line MN.

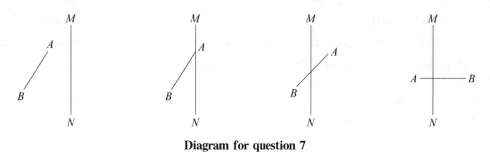

Diagram for question 7

8 Draw △A′B′C′ that is symmetric to △ABC with respect to the line MN.

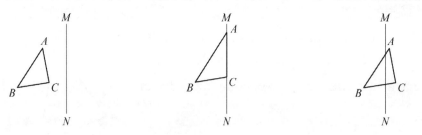

Diagram for question 8

9 Given △*ABC* and *A*′ is the image point of *A* about a reflection symmetry. Draw the line of symmetry and △*A*′*B*′*C*′ that is the image of △*ABC* under the reflection over the line.

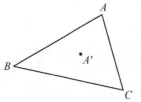

Diagram for question 9

10 Given two figures are reflectively symmetric, draw the mirror line *l* and fill in the blanks below.

(a)

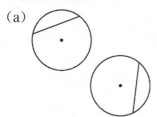

(b)

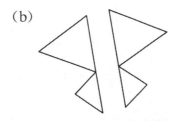

Diagram for question 10

(c) If two figures are symmetric about a line, there are two methods to find their line of symmetry. The first method is to get a pair of line segments each connecting a point in the original figure and its image point, locate the _____ of the two line segments, and then draw a line connecting the _____ , which is the line of symmetry. The second method is to get a line segment joining a point in the original figure and its image point, and then draw a line _____ and _____ the line segment.

Unit test 5

1　In the following, the figure with the greatest number of lines of symmetry is (　　).

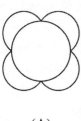　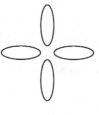　　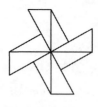

　(A)　　　　　　　　(B)　　　　　　　　(C)　　　　　　　　(D)

2　In the following, the figure that must have reflection symmetry is (　　).
　A. any two points　　　　　　　B. a triangle
　C. a parallelogram　　　　　　　D. a pentagon

3　In the following, the figure that has both point symmetry and reflection symmetry is (　　).
　A. an angle
　B. an equilateral triangle
　C. a square
　D. a hexagon

4　In the following, the number of figures that can be viewed as both the result of a rotation and that of a reflection is (　　).

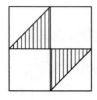　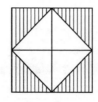　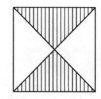　

　A. 1　　　　　　B. 2　　　　　　C. 3　　　　　　D. 4

B. Fill in the blanks

5 When a figure is translated, rotated, or flipped, these transformations have one common property; that is, the _____ and _____ of the figure remain the same.

6 If a square is rotated around its centre for at least _____ degrees, then the resulting figure will coincide with the square itself.

7 A parallelogram can be obtained by rotating a triangle around the midpoint of one side for _____ degrees.

8 Point symmetry _____ also rotational symmetry. (Choose 'is' or 'is not' to fill in.)

9 The star can be viewed as a result of a quadrilateral through rotating _____ times. Each time, the angle of rotation is at least _____ degrees, therefore it has _____ symmetry.

Diagram for question 9

10 If a figure has line symmetry, then the line of symmetry is _____ to and _____ any line segment joining a point with its image point.

11 As shown in the diagram, if $\triangle ABC$ is rotated around point A to the position of $\triangle ADE$, then the angle that must be equal to $\angle BAD$ is _____.

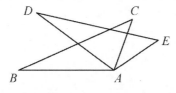

Diagram for question 11

12 The diagram shows a square $ABCD$, points E and F are on sides BC and CD respectively, and $\angle EAF = 45°$. If the right-angled $\triangle ADF$ is rotated $90°$ clockwise around point A to the position of $\triangle ABG$, then $\triangle AGE$ can be rotated _____ degrees _____ around point A to the position of $\triangle AFH$.

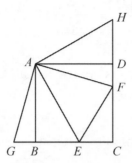

Diagram for question 12

13 As shown in the diagram, point E is on side BC of square $ABCD$, F lies on the extension of side AB beyond B, and $\triangle AEB$ can be rotated a certain number of degrees to coincide with $\triangle CFB$. Then line segments AE and CF are _____.

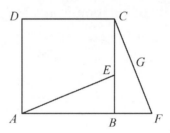

Diagram for question 13

C. Construction questions

14 Construct the image of quadrilateral $ABCD$ after a reflection about the line l.

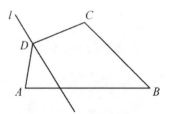

Diagram for question 14

15 Using the diagram below, first translate the figure in the square grid so point A moves to point A', and then rotate it for $180°$ around point A'. Draw the images of the figure after the translation and rotation, respectively.

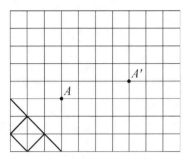

Diagram for question 15

16 Draw the image point over a transformation.

(a) The following figure has rotational symmetry about O_1. Draw the image A_1 of point A.

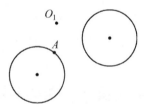

(b) The following figure has point symmetry. Draw the image A_2 of point A.

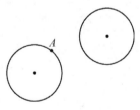

(c) The following figure has rotational symmetry about O_1. Draw the image B_1 of the point B.

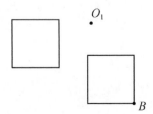

(d) The following figure has point symmetry. Draw the image B_2 of point B.

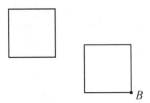

D. Questions that require solutions

17 The diagram shows $\triangle ABC$ on a square grid.

(a) Draw $\triangle A_1 B_1 C_1$ that is symmetric to $\triangle ABC$ about line l;

(b) Draw $\triangle A_2 B_2 C_2$ that is symmetric to $\triangle ABC$ about the point O;

(c) If it is a 2-cm square grid, find the area of $\triangle ABC$;

(d) Can $\triangle A_2 B_2 C_2$ be obtained by translating $\triangle A_1 B_1 C_1$? How about by rotating $\triangle A_1 B_1 C_1$? By what kind of transformation can one triangle be generated from the other?

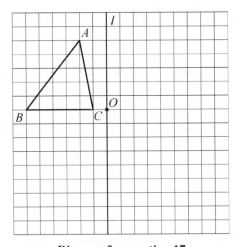

Diagram for question 17

18 The diagram shows that in $\triangle ABC$, D is the midpoint of BC, E and F lie on AB and AC respectively, and $\angle EDF = 90°$.

(a) Draw the image point F_1 of point F after a reflection over line ED;

(b) Joining BF_1 and DF_1, what kind of relationship do $\triangle BF_1D$ and $\triangle CFD$ have? Give your reason.

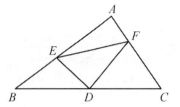

Diagram for question 18

19 As shown in the diagram, squares $ABDE$ and $ACFG$ are drawn outwards on sides AB and AC of $\triangle ABC$, respectively. Explain after what transformation line segment BG coincides with line segment EC? Do $\triangle ABG$ and $\triangle AEC$ always exist? If not, explain under what conditions they exist.

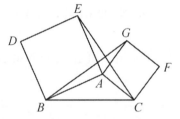

Diagram for question 19

20 As shown in the diagram, point C lies on line segment BE. On the same side of BE we draw equilaterals $\triangle ABC$ and $\triangle DCE$, then we can see that $\triangle ACE$ can coincide with $\triangle BCD$ after a rotation.

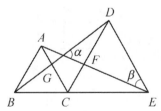

Diagram for question 20

(a) Write down the angle and direction of the rotation.

(b) In the diagram, what pairs of triangles can coincide with each other after the rotation?

(c) If $\beta = 40°$, then $\angle BDE = $ _____.

Chapter 6   Learning more about cubes and cuboids

6.1   The surface area of a cube

 Learning objective

Understand and use properties of faces of cubes and solve related problems

A. Multiple choice questions

1 The correct statement about all the faces of a cube is (   ).
A. All are squares.
B. Not all are squares.
C. Some are squares and some are rectangles.
D. None of the above is correct.

2 The net of a cube consists of (   ) identical squares.
A. 4   B. 5   C. 6   D. 8

3 Among the following figures，those shown in (   ) are nets of cubes.（Choose all the correct answers.）

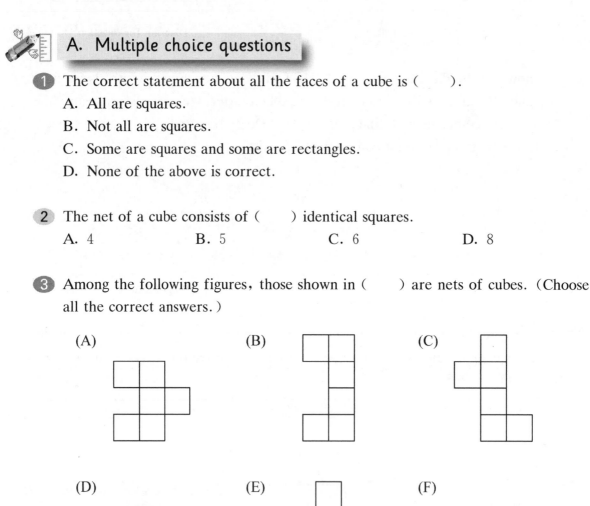

(A)   (B)   (C)

(D)   (E)   (F)

B. Fill in the blanks

4 Given that the length of the edge of a cube is a cm, then the sum of the lengths of the edges is _____ cm and the surface area of the cube is _____ cm^2. If $a =$ 2 cm, then the sum of the lengths of the edges is _____ cm, and the surface area is _____ cm^2.

5 Find the surface areas of the following figures.

(a)

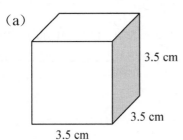

3.5 cm
3.5 cm
3.5 cm

Answer: _____

(b)

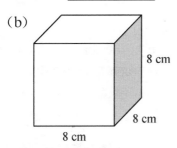

8 cm
8 cm
8 cm

Answer: _____

6 The diagram shows a cube with edge length 5 cm. The cube is made up of 1 cm^3 cubic blocks. Paint the surface area red, and then put it back into 1 cm^3 cubic blocks:

(a) There are _____ blocks with one face painted.

(b) There are _____ blocks with two faces painted.

(c) There are _____ blocks with three faces painted.

(d) There are _____ blocks with no faces painted.

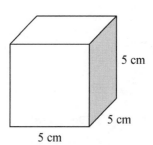

5 cm
5 cm
5 cm

Diagram for question 6

7 If the perimeter of the bottom face of a cube is 48 cm, then the surface area is _____ cm^2.

C. Questions that require solutions

8 The sum of the lengths of all the edges of a cube is 600 cm. What is its surface area?

9 The packing workshop of a food factory needs to produce a batch of cubic paper boxes with edge length 40 cm. At least how many square metres of cardboard is needed to make 125 of the cubic paper boxes?

10 A roll of ribbon can wrap 6 cubic gift boxes, as shown in the diagram. The edge length of each cube is 20 cm and the ribbon needed for each knot is 30 cm long. What is the length of the roll of ribbon?

Diagram for question 10

11 A cubic wooden box with edge length 1.5 m is to be painted. If each square metre needs 0.5 kg of paint, how many kilograms of paint is needed to paint the wooden box?

6.2 The surface area of a cuboid

 Learning objective

Understand and use properties of faces of cuboids and solve related problems

 A. Multiple choice questions

1 The net of a cuboid consists of (　　).

  A. 6 squares

  B. 6 rectangles

  C. 2 squares and 4 rectangles

  D. 4 squares and 2 rectangles

2 In the following figures, those shown in (　　) are not nets of cuboids.

(A)　　　　　　　　(B)　　　　　　　　(C)　　　　　　　　(D)

B. Fill in the blanks

3 The length of the cuboid in the diagram is _____ cm, the width is _____ cm and the height is _____ cm. The sum of the areas of the top and bottom faces is _____ cm^2, the sum of the areas of the front and rear faces is _____ cm^2, and the sum of the areas of the left and right faces is _____ cm^2. The surface area of the cuboid is _____ cm^2.

4

13　　3

Diagram for question 3

4 Find the surface areas of the figures below.

(a)

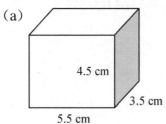

4.5 cm

3.5 cm

5.5 cm

(b)

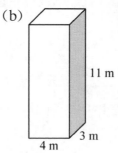

11 m

4 m

3 m

Answer: _____

Answer: _____

 C. Questions that require solutions

5 The length of a cuboid wooden box is 2.5 m, the width is 2.1 m and the height is 1.8 m. At least how many square metres of board are needed to make the wooden box?

6 A cuboid is large enough to be cut into two cubes with edge length 4 cm. How many square centimetres is the surface area of the cuboid?

7 To make a ventilation duct with a length of 130 cm and both width and height of 20 cm, at least how many square centimetres of iron sheet is needed?

8 The sum of the edge lengths of a cuboid and a cube are equal. The cuboid has a length of 5 cm, a width of 3 cm and a height of 1 cm. What are the surface areas of the cuboid and the cube?

9 The length, width and height of a cuboid wooden drawer are 74 cm, 65 cm and 15 cm, respectively. At least how many square centimetres of wood board are needed to make 20 such drawers?

6.3 Change of surface areas (1)

Learning objective

Solve problems involving change of surface areas of cubes and cuboids

A. Multiple choice questions

1 Four identical cubes with edge length 1 cm are put together in a row to form a cuboid. The surface area of the cuboid is (　　).

A. 16 cm^2　　　　B. 18 cm^2　　　　C. 20 cm^2　　　　D. 24 cm^2

2 When a cubic wooden block with edge length 10 cm is cut into three cuboids with the same volume, the surface area from the cube to the three cuboids increases by (　　) cm^2.

A. 200　　　　B. 400　　　　C. 600　　　　D. 800

3 When 6 identical cubes are put together to form a cuboid, the surface area from the 6 cubes to the cuboid (　　).

A. increases　　　　　　　　B. decreases

C. remains unchanged　　　　D. cannot be decided

B. Fill in the blanks

4 Fill in the table.

Cuboids by combining identical cubes with edge length 1 cm				
How many faces are hidden after combination?				
Sum of the surface areas of the identical cubes (cm^2)				
The surface area of the combined cuboids (cm^2)				

⑤ Each figure below is made up of identical cubes with edge length 2 cm. How much surface area is reduced from before to after the combination?

(a)

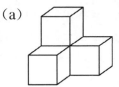

(b)

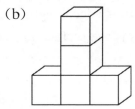

Answer: _____

Answer: _____

C. Questions that require solutions

⑥ The cuboid in the diagram is 150 cm long. When it is cut into two identical cubes, by how many more square centimetres has the sum of the surface areas of the two cubes increased, compared with the surface area of the original cuboid?

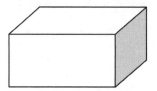

Diagram for question 6

⑦ When 3 identical cubes are put together to form a cuboid, the surface area of the cuboid is 84 cm². How many square centimetres is the surface area of each cube?

⑧ Eight identical cubic blocks with edge length 1 cm can be combined to form a cuboid in 3 different shapes. What is the maximum surface area of the combined cuboid? What is the minimum surface area of the combined cuboid?

9 There is a cubic wooden block with edge length 8 cm.

(a) If a cube with edge length 1 cm at a vertex is cut off, how many square centimetres is the surface area of the remaining solid figure?

(b) If a cube with edge length 1 cm is cut off in the middle of an edge, how many square centimetres is the surface area of the remaining solid figure?

(c) If a cube with edge length 1 cm is cut off in the middle of a face, how many square centimetres is the surface area of the remaining solid figure?

6.4　Change of surface areas (2)

Learning objective

Solve problems involving change of surface areas of cubes and cuboids

A. Multiple choice questions

1 The edge length of a cube is 5 cm. If the cube is divided into three identical small cuboids, the surface area is increased by (　　) cm^2.

A. 50　　　　　　　　　　　　B. 75

C. 100　　　　　　　　　　　 D. 150

2 A cuboid is 5 cm long, 4 cm wide and 3 cm high. Paint all the 6 surfaces of the cuboid red first, and then cut it into small cubes with edge length 1 cm. There are (　　) small cubes without the red paint.

A. 6　　　　　　B. 8　　　　　　C. 22　　　　　　D. 24

B. Fill in the blanks

3 Two identical cuboids with the dimensions 5 cm by 4 cm by 2 cm are put together to form a large cuboid. The maximum surface area of this cuboid is _____ cm^2 and the minimum surface area is _____ cm^2.

4 Eight identical small cubes are combined to form a large cube. The surface area of the combined cube is _____ times the surface area of the small cube.

5 The areas of the bottom face, the front face and the right side face of a cuboid are 12 cm^2, 8 cm^2 and 6 cm^2, respectively. The length of the cuboid is _____ cm, the width is _____ cm and the height is _____ cm. The volume is _____ cm^3.

6 A cube with edge length 9 cm can be divided into _____ small cubes with edge length 3 cm. The total surface area of all the small cubes is _____ more than the surface area of the original cube.

7 64 identical small cubes with edge length 1 cm are combined to form a large cube. The surface area of the large cube is _____ cm^2.

C. Questions that require solutions

8 The surface area of a cube is 216 cm^2. When the length of one edge is reduced by half so it becomes a cuboid, by how many square centimetres is the surface area reduced?

9 If a cuboid with length 160 cm and height 60 cm is cut horizontally into two small cuboids, the total surface area will increase by 16 000 cm^2. Find the surface area and volume of the original cuboid.

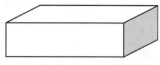

Diagram for question 9

10 The height of a cube is increased by 3 cm so it becomes a cuboid, while the bottom face remains unchanged. If the surface area from the cube to the cuboid is increased by 96 cm^2, find the surface area of the cube.

11 A swimming pool is 50 m long, 20 m wide and 2.5 m deep. If the four side walls and the bottom are to be tiled, how many square metres of the area is to be tiled? If the side length of a square tile is 0.3 m, then how many of the tiles are needed?

12 A square-shaped iron sheet has the dimensions $120 \text{ cm} \times 120 \text{ cm}$. If a square with length 20 cm is cut off from each of the four corners, the remaining part of the sheet is exactly enough to be folded into a cuboid without a cover. What is the volume of the cuboid? (Ignore the thickness of the iron sheet.)

13 A cuboid is 5 cm long, 4 cm wide and 3 cm high. Four of the identical cuboids are combined to make a large cuboid. What is the surface area of the large cuboid? (Write all the possible results.)

6.5 Different parts of a cuboid

Learning objective

Use properties of faces, surfaces, edges and vertices of cuboids to solve problems in 3-D

A. Multiple choice questions

1 All the 12 edges of a cuboid can be classified into ( ) groups so the edges in each group have the same length.

A. 2　　　　　B. 3　　　　　C. 4　　　　　D. 6

2 In a cuboid, there are ( ) edges that pass through each vertex.

A. 1　　　　　B. 2　　　　　C. 3　　　　　D. 4

3 If a cuboid is not a cube, then it has at most ( ) square faces.

A. 0　　　　　B. 2　　　　　C. 4　　　　　D. 6

B. Fill in the blanks

4 A cuboid has _____ vertices, _____ edges and _____ faces.

5 The diagram shows a cuboid. The edges that have the same length as EF are _____ and the face that is opposite to the face $AEHD$ is _____ .

6 The diagram shows a cuboid with $AB = 4\,\text{cm}$, $DA = 5\,\text{cm}$ and $AE = 3\,\text{cm}$. The sum of the edges of the cuboid is _____ cm, the area of the face $DCGH$ is _____ cm² and $BC = $ _____ cm.

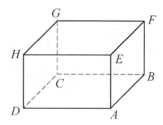

Diagram for questions 5 and 6

7 A cuboid is _____ a cube. A cube is _____ a cuboid. (Choose 'definitely', 'not necessarily' or 'definitely not' to fill in.)

8 A cuboid is cut evenly into five cubes and the surface area is increased by 40 cm^2. The original surface area of the cuboid was _____ cm^2.

C. Questions that require solutions

9 The diagram shows a rectangular piece of paper with the dimensions $8 \text{ cm} \times 6 \text{ cm}$. A square with side length 1.5 cm was cut off from each of the four corners. It was then folded along the dotted lines into a cuboid box without the top. Find the volume of the cuboid box.

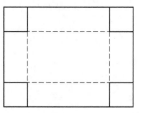

Diagram for question 9

10 In a cuboid, the lengths of three edges sharing a common vertex are 5 cm, 6 cm and 7 cm. Find the sum of all the edge lengths of the cuboid.

11 The diagram shows an object made up of three cubes. How many faces does the object have? What is its surface area?

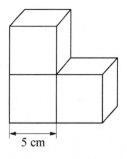

5 cm

Diagram for question 11

12 A cuboid measuring 8 cm × 5 cm × 6 cm is cut into a cube that has the maximum possible volume. Find the volume of the part that was cut off.

13 The sum of all the edge lengths of a cuboid is 108 cm and the ratio of the length: width: height is 4 : 3 : 2. What is the volume of the cuboid?

6.6 Properties of cuboids: relationship between edges

Learning objective

Understand and use properties and relationships between edges of cuboids to solve problems in 3-D

A. Multiple choice questions

1. All the 12 edges of a cuboid can be classified into (　　) groups so the edges in each group are parallel to each other.

   A. 2　　　　　　　　B. 3　　　　　　　　C. 4　　　　　　　　D. 6

2. Among the 12 edges of a cuboid, there are (　　) pairs of edges that are parallel to each other.

   A. 12　　　　　　　B. 16　　　　　　　C. 18　　　　　　　D. 24

3. Among the following statements, the correct one is (　　).

   A. In a cuboid, there are 4 edges that pass through each vertex.

   B. In a cuboid, there are 4 edges that intersect each edge.

   C. In a cuboid, there are 4 edges that are parallel to each edge.

   D. In a cuboid, there are 4 edges that are equal to each edge.

B. Fill in the blanks

4. In general, if line AB and line CD are on the same plane and have only one common point, then the two lines are called _____ lines.

5. In general, if line AB and line CD are on the same plane and have no common point, then the two lines are called _____ lines.

6. The diagram shows a cuboid $ABCD$-$EFGH$. The edges that are parallel to edge CD are _____ ; the edges that intersect edge CD are _____ ; the edges that are neither intersecting nor parallel to edge CD are _____ .

   (Note: In a 3-D space, two lines that do not intersect and are not parallel to each other are called 'skew lines'.)

177

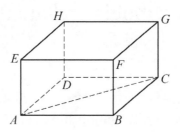

Diagram for questions 6 and 7

7 As shown in the diagram, among the 12 edges of the cuboid $ABCD$–$EFGH$, there are _____ edges that are parallel to AC; there are _____ edges that intersect AC; there are _____ edges that are neither intersecting nor parallel to AC.

C. Questions that require solutions

8 In a cuboid, the lengths of the 3 edges that have a common vertex are 5 cm, 6 cm and 3 cm. Find the volume of the cuboid.

9 The diagram shows the figure obtained after a rectangular piece of paper $ABCD$ is folded first and then unfolded. Write the lines as indicated.

(a) The line(s) parallel to line DF.

(b) The line(s) parallel to line EF.

(c) The line(s) intersecting line EF.

(d) The line(s) neither intersecting nor parallel to line BE.

(e) The line(s) neither intersecting nor parallel to line BC.

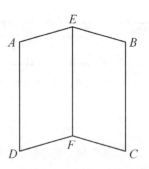

Diagram for question 9

10 As shown in the diagram, write the relationship between the lines indicated.

(a) *DH* and *BG*

(b) *EG* and *BG*

(c) *AC* and *EG*

(d) *DC* and *EG*

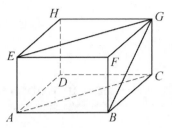

Diagram for question 10

11 The areas of three neighbouring faces of a cuboid are 6 cm², 8 cm² and 12 cm². Find the volume of the cuboid.

12 When a corner of a cuboid is cut off, how many edges are there in the cuboid? (Sketch a diagram to explain.)

6.7 Properties of cuboids: relationship between edges and faces

Learning objective

Understand and use properties and relationships between edges and faces of cuboids to solve problems in 3-D

A. Multiple choice questions

1 In the following statements about a cuboid, (   ) of them is/are correct.

① Each edge is perpendicular to two faces.

② Each face is perpendicular to two edges.

③ If an edge and a face have only one common point, then the edge is perpendicular to the face.

④ For three edges sharing the same vertex, any two of them are perpendicular to each other.

A. 1   B. 2

C. 3   D. 4

2 In the following four figures, (   ) of them can be folded into a cuboid.

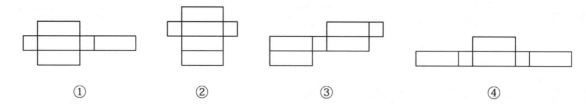

①   ②   ③   ④

A. 1   B. 2

C. 3   D. 4

B. Fill in the blanks

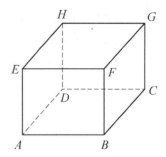

3 In the cuboid shown in the diagram, edge *BF* and plane *ABCD* are _____ .

4 In the cuboid shown in the diagram, edges _____ are perpendicular to plane *BCGF*.

5 In the cuboid shown in the diagram, planes _____ _____ are perpendicular to edge *EH*.

Diagram for questions 3, 4 and 5

C. Questions that require solutions

6 The diagram shows a cuboid: *AB* is 6 cm, *BC* is 3 cm and *BF* is 2 cm. Find the sum of all the edges that are perpendicular to plane *ABFE*.

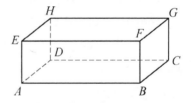

Diagram for question 6

7 The base of a cuboid is a square and its 4 side faces can exactly form a square with side length 8 cm. Find the volume of the cuboid.

8 The diagram shows a cuboid. The sum of the lengths of the edges that are perpendicular to plane *ABCD* is 12 cm, and the sum of the areas of the planes that are perpendicular to plane *ABCD* is 54 cm. Find the sum of the lengths of all the edges of the cuboid.

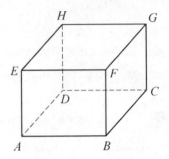

Diagram for question 8

9 After the surface of a large cuboid was painted, the cuboid was cut into a number of small identical cubes. As a result, there were exactly 12 of the small cubes containing two painted faces. What is the minimum number of the small cubes that the cuboid was cut into?

10 The diagram shows a cuboid and length *AB* is 5 cm. The sum of the lengths of the edges that are parallel to plane *BCGF* is 18 cm and the sum of the lengths of the edges that are perpendicular to plane *ABFE* is 24 cm. Find the surface area and the volume of the cuboid.

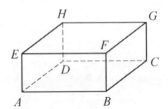

Diagram for question 10

6.8 Properties of cuboids: relationship between faces

Learning objective

Understand and use properties and relationships between faces of cuboids to solve problems in 3-D

A. Multiple choice questions

1. For each face of a cuboid, there is/are (   ) face(s) that are perpendicular to it.

   A. 0   B. 1   C. 2   D. 4

2. For each face of a cuboid, there is/are (   ) face(s) that are parallel to it.

   A. 0   B. 1   C. 2   D. 4

3. There are (   ) pairs of faces that are perpendicular to each other in a cuboid.

   A. 4   B. 8   C. 12   D. 24

4. There are (   ) pairs of planes that are parallel to each other in a cuboid.

   A. 1   B. 2   C. 3   D. 4

5. In a cuboid, two faces that are perpendicular to each other must (   ).

   A. have a common point   B. have the same perimeter

   C. have the same area   D. both be squares

B. Fill in the blanks

6. If planes α and β are perpendicular to each other, then it is denoted as _____.

7. If planes α and β are parallel to each other, then it is denoted as _____.

> A **plane** is a flat surface that extends infinitely in two dimensions. It has no thickness.

8 In the cuboid, as shown in the diagram, the plane(s) that is/are perpendicular to plane *ABCD* is/are

_____ .

9 In the cuboid, as shown in the diagram, the plane(s) that is/are perpendicular to plane *ADHE* is/are

_____ .

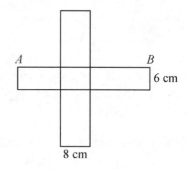

Diagram for questions 8 and 9

 ## C. Questions that require solutions

10 The diagram shows the net of a cuboid box and the length of *AB* is 36 cm. Using the measurements indicated in the diagram, find the volume of the cuboid.

A _____ *B*

6 cm

8 cm

Diagram for question 10

11 The diagram shows a cuboid. Its top, front and right faces are labelled 1, 2 and 3. The opposite faces of 1, 2 and 3 are labelled 4, 5 and 6.

(a) Find the product of numbers labelled on the planes that are perpendicular to the plane labelled 3.

(b) Find the product of 2 and the number labelled on the plane that is not perpendicular to the plane labelled 2.

(c) If the sum of the numbers labelled on the planes that are perpendicular to a plane is 14, find the number on the plane.

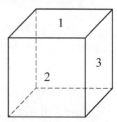

Diagram for question 11

12 The diagram shows a cuboid wooden block, AB is 40 cm and $AQ : BQ = 1 : 3$. Plane $QPNM$ is parallel to plane $ADHE$. If the cuboid is cut along plane $QPNM$, then the surface area is increased by 1800 cm^2. Find the difference between the volumes of the two cuboids that are created after the cutting.

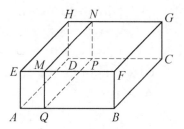

Diagram for question 12

Unit test 6

A. Multiple choice questions

1. Use a piece of iron wire with length 48 cm to form the largest possible cube. The edge length of the cube is (　　).

   A. 4 cm　　　　　B. 8 cm　　　　　C. 12 cm　　　　　D. 16 cm

2. The two neighbouring faces of a cuboid (　　).

   A. are perpendicular　　　　　　　B. are parallel

   C. may be perpendicular or parallel　　D. cannot be determined

3. The incorrect statement of the following is (　　).

   A. In a cuboid, the area of the two faces that are opposite to each other is the same.

   B. In a cuboid, each edge is perpendicular to two faces.

   C. In a cuboid there are 8 vertices, 12 edges and 6 faces.

   D. In a cuboid, edges are either parallel or intersecting.

4. There is/are (　　) face(s) that are parallel to a face in a cuboid.

   A. 1　　　　　　B. 2　　　　　　C. 3　　　　　　D. 4

5. In the diagram, the figure on the left shows a cube. In the four figures on its right, (　　) is a net of the cube.

   (A)　　　　　　(B)　　　　　　(C)　　　　　　(D)

   Diagram for question 5

B. Fill in the blanks

6. When looking at a cuboid, you can see _____ face(s) at most and _____ face(s) at least.

186

7 In a cuboid, any two edges have _____ intersecting point(s) at most and _____ intersecting point(s) at least.

8 In a cuboid, there are at least _____ edges with the same length.

9 In a cuboid, there are _____ edges that are perpendicular to a face.

10 As shown in the diagram, there are _____ edges hidden and _____ planes hidden from view.

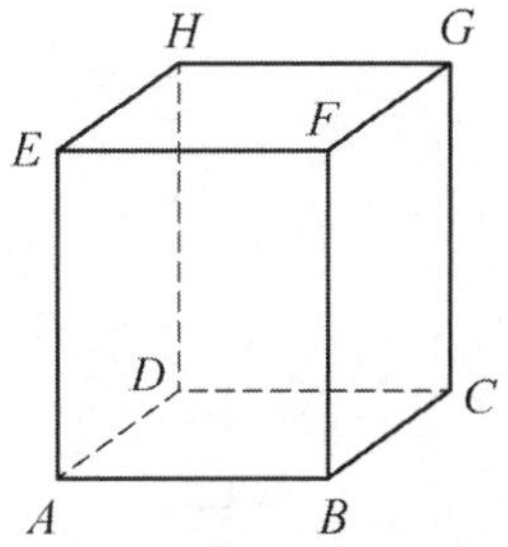

11 The diagram shows a cuboid $ABCD-EFGH$. The edges that have the same length as HG are _____ , the face that is opposite to plane $ABFE$ is _____ .

12 As shown in the diagram, in cuboid $ABCD-EFGH$, the edges that are parallel to edge AB are _____ , the edges that intersect edge BC are _____ and the edges that are neither intersecting nor parallel to the edge BF are _____ .

Diagram for questions 10 – 15

13 As shown in the diagram, the planes that are parallel to the edge EF are _____ .

14 As shown in the diagram, there are _____ edges that are perpendicular to edge AD with an intersecting point.

15 As shown in the diagram, there are _____ planes that are perpendicular to plane $BCGF$.

16 When a cuboid is cut into two cuboids, the number of edges is increased by _____ .

17 In a cuboid, if the sum of the length, width and height is 12 cm, then the sum of all the edges of the cuboid is _____ cm.

18 A cube is placed on the ground. Its side length is 2 cm. The sum of the edges that are parallel to the ground is _____ cm.

19 Given that the ratio of the length, width and height of a cuboid is $5 : 4 : 3$, use a piece of iron wire with length 48 cm to form a model of the cuboid. The surface area of the cuboid is _____ cm^2.

C. Questions that require solutions

20 The diagram shows a piece of paper. Can it be folded up into a cubic box? If so, then shade the plane that is perpendicular to plane C in the cubic box formed.

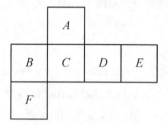

Diagram for question 20

21 The diagram shows a cuboid with the dimensions 6 cm by 4 cm by 5 cm. Inside the cuboid, a small cuboid that has a square base with side length 2 cm is removed. If it is then immersed into a colouring liquid, what will be the area of the coloured faces?

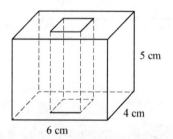

Diagram for question 21

22 The edges of a cuboid paper box without the top are 2 cm, 3 cm and 4 cm, respectively. What is the surface area of the paper box?

23 Given a cuboid wooden block, after two cuboids with the lengths 2 cm and 5 cm respectively are cut off from the left and right sides of the block, it will become a cube, and the surface area will be reduced by 84 cm².
(a) Find the edge length of the cube.
(b) Find the volume of the original cuboid.

24 Diagram (1) below shows a rectangular piece of paper with the dimensions 10 cm by 6 cm. It is cut into five pieces to form a cuboid container without a top, as shown in diagram (2). Find the length, width, height and volume of the container.

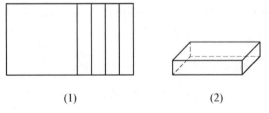

(1)   (2)

Diagram for question 24

Chapter 7 Algebraic expressions: concepts, addition and subtraction

7.1 Using letters to represent numbers

 Learning objective

Interpret and use letters to represent numbers in algebraic expressions

 A. Multiple choice questions

1 Among the following expressions that use letters, there is/are (   ) expression(s) written properly as the final answer(s).

① $1 \times x^2 y$ ② $ab \div c^2$ ③ $2 \times (a+b)$ ④ $ab \times 2$ ⑤ $1\frac{2}{3}xy$ ⑥ $\frac{7a}{4}$

A. 1   B. 2   C. 3   D. 4

2 John has x pounds as a deposit. The deposit David has is £2 more than half of John's. The deposit David has is (   ) pounds.

A. $\frac{1}{2}(x+2)$ B. $\frac{1}{2}(x-2)$ C. $\frac{1}{2}x+2$ D. $\frac{1}{2}x-2$

3 If, after a discount of $x\%$, the sale price of a product is a pounds, then the original price was (   ) pounds.

A. $\frac{ax}{100}$ B. $a\left(1+\frac{x}{100}\right)$ C. $\frac{100a}{x}$ D. $\dfrac{a}{1-\frac{x}{100}}$

 B. Fill in the blanks

4 The mass of water in the human body is approximately 70% of the total mass of the human body. If someone has a weight of m kg, then the mass of the water in the body is approximately _____ .

5 Use the letters a, b and c to express the distributive law of multiplication over addition: _____ .

6 Use the letters a, b and m $(b \neq 0, m \neq 0)$ to express the basic property of fractions: _____ .

7 In a three-digit number, if the digit in its ones place is a, the digit in its tens place is b, and the digit in its hundreds place is c, then the three-digit number can be expressed as _____ .

C. Questions that require solutions

8 The perimeter of a rectangle is l, and its length is a. Find its width.

9 A notebook costs £8 and a ballpoint pen costs £3. If you buy a notebooks and b pens, and you pay £100, how much change do you get?

10 A maths class consists of 12 boys and 18 girls. In a maths test, the average score of the boys is a, and the average score of the girls is b. What is the average score of the whole class in the test?

11 Andrew walks 1000 m from home to school. His speed going to school one day was a m per hour and on the way home, his speed was b m per hour. How much time in total did he spend going to and from school on the day?

12 Look at the diagram below and continue the matchstick pattern to set up equilateral triangles.

(a) How many matchsticks are needed to set up 5 triangles?

(b) How many matchsticks are needed to set up n triangles?

      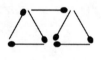

  1   2   3

7.2 Introduction to algebraic expressions

 Learning objective

Identify algebraic expressions; use and interpret related notations

 A. Multiple choice questions

1 Among the following expressions, there is/are ( ) algebraic expressions.

① $3xy^2$ ② $2\pi r$ ③ $S = \pi r^2$ ④ b ⑤ $5 + 1 > 2$ ⑥ $\dfrac{ab}{2}$

A. 3   B. 4   C. 5   D. 6

2 Among the following algebraic expressions used, the incorrect one is ( ).

A. $2x + 3y$ means the sum of $2x$ and $3y$.

B. $\dfrac{5x}{2y}$ means the quotient of $5x$ divided by $2y$.

C. $9 - \dfrac{1}{3}y$ means the difference of 9 subtracted by $\dfrac{1}{3}$ of y.

D. $a^2 + b^2$ means the square of the sum of a and b.

3 Among the following sentences describing the quantitative relationship in $3a - 15$, the incorrect one is ( ).

A. the difference of 3 times a and 15

B. the sum of $3a$ and -15

C. 3 times a minus 15

D. 3 times the difference of a and 15

 B. Fill in the blanks

4 Use an algebraic expression to represent: the difference of m and twice n is _____.

5 Use an algebraic expression to represent: twice the difference of m and n is _____.

6 Use an algebraic expression to represent: the difference of a and b squared is _____.

7 Use an algebraic expression to represent: the square of the difference of a and b is

_____ .

8 To represent the sum of $\frac{1}{3}$ of x and 4, the algebraic expression is _____ .

9 To represent $\frac{1}{3}$ of the sum of x and 4, the algebraic expression is: _____ .

10 To represent the product of the difference of x and 4 and the reciprocal of 3, the algebraic expression is _____ .

C. Questions that require solutions

11 The monthly interest rate for a bank deposit was $x\%$. Maria made an initial deposit of £1000 on 1 March 2014, and withdrew the principal (that is, the initial deposit) and all the accumulated interest on 1 August 2016. How much did she get in total?

12 On a sports ground, a circular track is 400 m long. Two runners, A and B, started running from the same place but in opposite directions around the track. The speed of A was x m per second, and the speed of B was y m per second. After how long did they meet for the first time?

⑬ The cost price of a product was a pounds per item. The product was first sold at a retail price 40% higher than the cost price. After the peak selling season, it is then sold with a 20% discount for promotion purpose. Find the promotional price of the product.

14 There are a grams of 80% alcohol solution. After 10 grams of pure water is added, what is the percentage of alcohol in the new solution?

7.3 Values of algebraic expressions (1)

Learning objective

Substitute numerical values into formulae and algebraic expressions

A. Multiple choice questions

1 For $x = \dfrac{1}{3}$, the value of $9x^2 + x - 1$ is (　　).

    A. $8\dfrac{1}{3}$ B. $2\dfrac{2}{3}$ C. $2\dfrac{1}{3}$ D. $\dfrac{1}{3}$

2 For $x = 3$, and $y = -\dfrac{1}{2}$, the value of $\dfrac{2}{3}x - \dfrac{1}{2}y$ is (　　).

    A. $1\dfrac{3}{4}$ B. $2\dfrac{1}{4}$ C. $2\dfrac{3}{4}$ D. 3

3 For $x + y^2 = 1$, and $3x - 2y^2 = -2$, the value of $4x - y^2$ is (　　).

    A. -2 B. -1 C. 3 D. 6

B. Fill in the blanks

4 If $x = 5$ and $y = -\dfrac{1}{5}$, then $2xy + x =$ _____.

5 If $x = \dfrac{1}{3}$, then $\dfrac{5}{2x} =$ _____.

6 If $x = \dfrac{1}{2}$ and $x - y = 6\dfrac{1}{3}$, then $y =$ _____.

7 If $x + y = 9$ and $y = 10$, then $(x - y)^2 =$ _____.

8 If $a = 3$ and $b = 0.3$, then $\dfrac{\frac{1}{3}b}{2a} =$ _____.

⑨ If $a = 2$, $b = -1$ and $c = 3$, then $b^2 - 4ac =$ _____ .

⑩ If $a = -2$, $b = -3$ and $b^2 - 4ac = 4$, then $c =$ _____ .

C. Questions that require solutions

⑪ If $a^2 - a = 2015$, find the value of $(a^2 - a - 2016)^{2017}$.

⑫ The flowchart below shows the sequence of numerical calculation.

$$\boxed{\text{Input } x} \longrightarrow \boxed{\times \left(-\dfrac{2}{3}\right)} \longrightarrow \boxed{-2} \longrightarrow \boxed{\text{Output}}$$

When the input is $x = 6$ and $x = a$ respectively, what are the results of the output?

⑬ The conversion formula between the temperature in Fahrenheit (℉) and that in Celsius (℃) is: $℉ = ℃ \times \dfrac{9}{5} + 32$. When the temperature is $30℃$, how much is the temperature in Fahrenheit? If the temperature in Fahrenheit is x ℉, how much is the temperature in Celsius?

14 (a) When $a = 1$, $b = \dfrac{1}{3}$ and $a = \dfrac{3}{4}$, $b = \dfrac{1}{2}$, calculate the values of $a^2 - 2ab + b^2$ and $(a - b)^2$ respectively. Observe the values of the algebraic expressions. What do you find? What pattern can you guess?

(b) Using the pattern you identified, calculate:

$$101.23^2 - 2 \times 101.23 \times 1.23 + 1.23^2.$$

7.4 Values of algebraic expressions (2)

Learning objective

Substitute numerical values into formulae and algebraic expressions

A. Multiple choice questions

1. Given: $x = \left(-1 \div \dfrac{1}{2} \times 3 \times \dfrac{1}{6}\right)^3$, then the value of the algebraic expression $1 + x + x^2 + \cdots + x^{2016} + x^{2017}$ is (　　).

   A. 2017　　　　　B. 2016　　　　　C. 1　　　　　D. 0

2. The value of the algebraic expression $\dfrac{30}{6-a}$ could not be (　　).

   A. -1　　　　　B. 0　　　　　C. 1　　　　　D. 2

3. Given the value of $2x^2 - 4y^3 + 6$ is 1, then the value of the algebraic expression $x^2 - 2y^3 + 2$ is (　　).

   A. 3　　　　　B. -3　　　　　C. $\dfrac{1}{2}$　　　　　D. $-\dfrac{1}{2}$

B. Fill in the blanks

4. In m kg of 8% salt solution, it contains _____ kg of salt and _____ kg of water.

5. If a square has a perimeter of a, then its side length is _____, and its area is _____.

6. For $a = -2$ and $b = -1$, the value of the algebraic expression $a^3 + b^2$ is _____.

7. If $a = -b$, and c and d are reciprocals of each other, then $(a+b)^3 - (c \times d)^4 =$ _____.

8. If $x = -5$ and y is the least prime number, then the value of the algebraic expression $x^2 - xy$ is _____.

9 For $a = \dfrac{1}{2}$ and $b = \dfrac{2}{3}$, the value of the algebraic expression $2a - 5b$ is c, then the value of the algebraic expression $3c^2 - 2c$ is _____.

10 In the algebraic expression $5 - x^2$, when x is _____, the algebraic expression has the maximum value, which is equal to _____.

C. Questions that require solutions

11 Given: $(x - 2y)^2 + (3x - 2)^2 = 0$, find the value of $\dfrac{x}{y^2}$. (Hint: $a^2 \geqslant 0$ and when $a^2 = 0$, then $a = 0$.)

12 Given: $\dfrac{a - 2b}{a + 2b} = 4$, find the value of the algebraic expression

$$\dfrac{3(a - 2b)}{4(a + 2b)} + \dfrac{3(a + 2b)}{a - 2b}.$$

13 A factory has m kg of coal, and its original plan was to use a kg of coal per day. Now it uses b kg of coal less than planned per day. How many more days can the amount of coal last, as compared to the original plan? When $m = 10\,000$, $a = 250$, $b = 50$, how many days can the amount of coal last?

14 In a city, the water is charged using an escalating rate structure, and the tariff is as follows:

Amount of water used monthly	12 tons or less	More than 12 tons but not more than 18 tons	More than 18 tons
Rate (£/ton)	2.00	2.50	3.00

(a) Write the algebraic expressions to represent the water charges for $x \leqslant 12$, $12 < x \leqslant 18$, and $x > 18$, respectively.

(b) Three households used 10 tons, 16 tons, and 28 tons of water, respectively, in a particular month. How much should they pay, respectively?

7.5 Further concepts about algebraic expressions

 Learning objective

Understand and use concepts of algebraic expressions and related terms including coefficients, polynomials, degrees, descending or ascending orders, etc.

 A. Multiple choice questions

1 The coefficient of the single term algebraic expression (or monomial) $-5x^2y$ is (   ).

A. 0

B. 1

C. 5

D. -5

> If an algebraic expression has only one term like this, it is called a **monomial.** When an algebraic expression has two or more such terms, it is generally called a **polynomial.**

2 The degree of the monomial $3ax^2$ is (   ).

A. 1   B. 2

C. 3   D. 4

3 The algebraic expression $-\dfrac{1}{2}a + bx$ has (   ) terms.

A. 1   B. 2

C. 3   D. 4

4 Rearranging $a^3 - 3a + 10a^2 + 0.5$ in ascending power of a, the result is (   ).

A. $a^3 - 3a + 10a^2 + 0.5$ B. $a^3 - 3a + 10a^2 + 0.5$

C. $0.5 - 3a + 10a^2 + a^3$ D. $a^3 + 10a^2 - 3a + 0.5$

5 The algebraic expression $x^3 - 3x^2y + 4x^3y^2 + 5y^3$ is written (   ).

A. in ascending powers of x

B. in descending powers of x

C. in ascending powers of y

D. in descending powers of y

B. Fill in the blanks

6 Rearranging the algebraic expression $-2x^2+x-5+0.8x^3$ in descending powers of x, the result is _____ .

7 The monomial $-3ax^2$ has a coefficient _____ and degree _____ .

8 The monomial πr^2 has a coefficient _____ and degree _____ .

9 The algebraic expression $\frac{1}{2}xy^2-\frac{1}{3}x^2y^2+3$ has _____ terms, and the term with the highest degree is _____ . It has a degree of _____ .

In an algebraic expression, if the highest degree of all the terms is n, the algebraic expression is said to have a degree of n.

10 The algebraic expression $xy^2-3x^2y^3+4x^5-6$ has _____ terms, and the terms with the highest degree are _____ . They have a degree of _____ .

11 If the algebraic expression $1+x^m y+9y^m$ has a degree of 3, then $m=$ _____ .

C. Questions that require solutions

12 If $x^4 y^n+(m-3)x^5$ is a binomial of degree 5 in x and y, find the value of m and n. (Note: A binomial has two terms.)

13 If $x^{2m-3}y^4+xy^{m+1}$ has a degree of 5, find the value of m.

14 If $4a^2x^3 + ax^2 - 16x^3 - 2x^2 + 3x - 5$, in which only x is a variable, has a degree of 2, find the value of a.

15 Write an algebraic expression that satisfies the following four conditions simultaneously.
 ① The variables are x and y.
 ② The first term is constant.
 ③ It has 4 terms and a degree of 3.
 ④ The sum of the coefficients of all the terms is zero.

7.6 Simplifying algebraic expressions: collecting like terms (1)

Learning objective

Simplify and manipulate algebraic expressions by collecting like terms

A. Multiple choice questions

1. Among the following expressions, the like term of $-3x^2y^3$ is ( ).

   A. $-2xy$ B. $3x^2$ C. $5y^3$ D. $-7x^2y^3$

2. Among the following pairs of algebraic expressions, the pair of like terms is ( ).

   A. x^2y^3 and x^3y^2 B. $-xy^2$ and $-xy^2z$
   C. $10ab$ and $3ba$ D. $(-a)^3$ and $(-2)^3$

3. Among the following collections of like terms, the correct one is ( ).

   A. $5a-2a=3$ B. $2ab-2ba=0$
   C. $2a+3a=5a^2$ D. $2R+\pi R=2\pi R$

B. Fill in the blanks

4. If $x^{m-5}y^4$ and $\frac{1}{3}x^2y^{n+1}$ are like terms, then $m=$ _____, and $n=$ _____.

5. In the algebraic expression $3x^2y-2xy-3+4xy^2+6yx^2+7$, the like terms are

   _____ .

6. After collecting the like terms in the algebraic expressions $\frac{1}{2}x^2-x^2+x-1$, the resulting expression has _____ terms.

7. Collecting like terms: $-x-x=$ _____ .

8. Collecting like terms: $3x^2-2x+\frac{1}{3}x^2-\frac{2}{3}x=$ _____ .

9 Collecting like terms: $0.5x^2y + 1.5xy^2 - 0.1yx^2 + 3xy^2 - 1 =$ _____ .

10 Collecting like terms: $x^{n+1}y^2 - 4x^ny^n - 2y^2x^{n+1} - 5y^2x^{n+1} =$ _____ .

C. Questions that require solutions

11 If algebraic expressions $5x^{a+3b}y^5$ and $-3x^7y^{2a+3b}$ are like terms, find the values of a and b.

12 Given: $(x+3)^2 + (2x+y)^2 = 0$, simplify: $\frac{3}{4}x^2 - (3y - \frac{1}{4}x^2) + y$, and then find its value.

13 In a three-digit number, the digit in its tens place is the square of the digit in its hundreds place, and the number in its ones place is one less than twice the number in its hundreds place. Answer the following.

(a) If the number in the hundreds place is denoted by x, write down the expression, in descending powers of x, for the three-digit number.

(b) Find all the three-digit numbers satisfying the given conditions.

7.7 Simplifying algebraic expressions: collecting like terms (2)

Learning objective

Simplify and manipulate algebraic expressions by collecting like terms

A. Multiple choice questions

1 Collecting the like terms in $5(a-b)^2-7(a-b)^2-10(a-b)^2$, the result is (   ).

A. $-12(a-b)^2$ B. $-8(a-b)^2$ C. $-12a^2+12b^2$ D. $-8a^2+8b^2$

2 If $3x^{2a+b}y^b$ and $2x^{a+4}y^3$ are like terms, then the value of ab is (   ).

A. 1   B. 2   C. 3   D. 4

3 In a rectangle, one side has a length of $3a-b$, and the length of the other side is $a+3b$ longer. The perimeter of the rectangle is (   ).

A. $7a+b$ B. $14a+2b$ C. $4a+2b$ D. $8a+4b$

B. Fill in the blanks

4 If $ax^2+x^2-3x^2=2x^2$, then $a=$ _____.

5 If $(x^3-x)+(2-x^3+3x)=0$, then $x=$ _____.

6 When $c=0.2$, find the value: $\dfrac{2}{3}c^3+\dfrac{5}{6}c^3-\dfrac{1}{2}c^3=$ _____.

7 When $x=10$, find the value: $0.08x^4-0.12x^4+1.14x^4=$ _____.

8 If $A=4x^2-4$ and $B=2x+3$, then $\dfrac{A}{2}+B=$ _____.

9 After collecting the like terms in $-10x^2+13x^3-2+3x^3-4x^2-3+5x^2$, the result in descending powers of x; starting from the term with the highest degree of x, the term with the second highest degree of x, and so on, is _____.

C. Questions that require solutions

10 Simplify the algebraic expression $5.4x^2 - 0.6xy + 8y^2 - 1.4xy + 0.6x^2$, and then find its value for $x = 3$ and $y = \dfrac{1}{2}$.

11 If the sum of $3x^m y^n$ and $-3x^2 y^3$ is 0, find the value of the algebraic expression $2013(m+n)^3 - 2014(m+n)^3 + 2015(m-n)^3$.

12 In a school, there are three maths classes in Year 7. The number of students in the first class is x, the number in the second class is 3 more than that in the first class, and the number in the third class is 11 more than $\dfrac{2}{3}$ of the number in the first class. Find the number of all the students in Year 7.

13 Calculate the areas of the shaded regions in Diagrams (1) and (2), respectively, and then guess the area of the shaded region in Diagram (3). Give reasons for your answers.

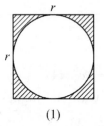 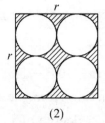 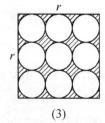

(1) (2) (3)

Diagram for question 13

7.8 Adding and subtracting algebraic expressions (1)

 Learning objective

Simplify and manipulate algebraic expressions by addition and subtraction, including removing brackets and collecting like terms

 A. Multiple choice questions

1. Among the following equations involving removing the brackets, the correct one is (　).
   A. $a-(b-c)=a-b-c$　　　　　B. $-a+(b-c)=-a-b+c$
   C. $-(a-b)+c=-a-b+c$　　　D. $-(a-b)-c=-a+b-c$

2. If the sum of a number and $a-2b-3c$ is 0, then the number can be expressed as (　).
   A. $a+2b+3c$　　B. $-a+2b+3c$　　C. $-a-2b-3c$　　D. $-a-2b+3c$

3. The result of $-(m+n)-(m-2n)$ is (　).
   A. $-2m-3n$　　B. $-2m-n$　　C. $-2m+n$　　D. n

 B. Fill in the blanks

4. Remove the brackets: $(x+2y)-(3a-4b) = $ _____ .

5. Remove the brackets: $-(x+2y)-(3a-4b) = $ _____ .

6. $(x+2y)-(3a-4b) = (x-3a)-($_____$)$.

7. $(x+2y)-(3a-4b) = (x+4b)+($_____$)$.

8. Simplify: $(13x-11y+10z)-(15x+10y-15z) = $ _____ .

9. Simplify: $\left(-\dfrac{5}{2}y^2\right)+(-4y^2)-\left(-\dfrac{7}{2}y^2\right)-(-3y) = $ _____ .

10. Simplify: $(x^3-y^3)-(x^3+y^3)+(y^3-1) = $ _____ .

C. Questions that require solutions

11 Given that the sum of the algebraic expressions $5x^2 - 2mxy - 13y^2 - x + y - 1$ and $4x^2 - 2xy - 10y^2 + x - y + 1$ does not have a term containing xy, find the value of m.

12 Simplify and then evaluate: $\frac{1}{2}a^2b^3 - \left(-\frac{1}{3}a^2b^3\right) - \left(\frac{-1}{4}a^2b^3\right)$ for $a = 2$ and $b = -1$.

13 Simplify and then evaluate: $(-a^3 - 3a^2 + 7a - 8) - (3a^3 - 2a^2 - 5a + 2) - (-a^3 - 2a^2 + 4)$, for $a = \frac{1}{2}$.

14 Explain why the sum of five consecutive positive integers is divisible by 5.

7.9 Adding and subtracting algebraic expressions (2)

Learning objective

Simplify and manipulate algebraic expressions by addition and subtraction, including removing brackets and collecting like terms

A. Multiple choice questions

1 $2a - 3$ is subtracted by another algebraic expression, and the result is $4a^2 + 5a - 6$. This algebraic expression is (   ).

A. $-4a^2 - 3a - 9$ B. $-4a^2 - 3a + 3$ C. $4a^2 + 3a - 3$ D. $4a^2 + 3a - 9$

2 An algebraic expression is added to $2a - 3$ and the result is $4a^2 + 5a - 6$. The algebraic expression is (   ).

A. $-4a^2 - 4a + 3$ B. $-4a^2 - 7a + 9$ C. $4a^2 + 3a - 3$ D. $4a^2 + 7a - 9$

3 An algebraic expression is subtracted by $2a - 3$, and the result is $4a^2 + 5a - 6$. The algebraic expression is (   ).

A. $-4a^2 - 4a + 3$ B. $-4a^2 - 7a + 9$ C. $4a^2 + 3a - 3$ D. $4a^2 + 7a - 9$

B. Fill in the blanks

4 $a - b + c + d = a - ($_____$)$.

5 $a^2 - b^2 - a + b = (a^2 - a) - ($_____$)$.

6 Simplify: $(-7x^3 - 2x^2) + (-3x^2 + 5x^3) = $_____.

7 Simplify: $-(-7x^3 - 2x^2) - (-3x^2 + 5x^3) = $_____.

8 The difference of $x^3 + 1$ and $-x^3 + 1$ is _____.

9 The sum of $-3a + 2b$ and $3b - 2a$ is _____.

10 The difference of $\frac{1}{2}x^2 - 3xy + 4$ subtracted by $-\frac{1}{3}x^2 + xy - \frac{2}{3}$ is _____.

C. Questions that require solutions

11 Given: $A = -x^2 - 1$ and $A - B = -x^3 + 2x^2 - 5$, find B.

12 Given: $A = -\frac{5}{6}x^2 + \frac{4}{3}xy + \frac{3}{4}y^2$ and $B = \frac{1}{12}x^2 - \frac{1}{6}xy + \frac{1}{2}y^2$, find $A - 2B$.

13 Simplify: $5abc - \{2a^2b - [-5abc - (4ab^2 - a^2b)]\}$, and then find its value when a is the least positive integer and b is the greatest negative integer.

14 In a four-digit number, the digit in its thousands place and that in its tens places are the same, and the digit in its hundreds place and that in its ones place are the same. Explain why this four-digit number is divisible by 101.

7.10 Adding and subtracting algebraic expressions (3)

Learning objective

Simplify and manipulate algebraic expressions by addition and subtraction

A. Multiple choice questions

1 Among the following equations involving removing the brackets, the correct one is ( ).

A. $a - (2b - 3c) = a - 2b - 3c$

B. $a^3 - (2a^2 - 3a + 4) = a^3 - 2a^2 + 3a + 4$

C. $a + (2b - 3c) = a - 2b + 3c$

D. $a^2 - [2a - (-3b + c)] = a^2 - 2a - 3b + c$

2 Among the following algebraic expressions, ( ) is equal to $-2x^2y + 3xy^2 - xy - x^3 + y^3$.

A. $-(2x^2y - 3xy^2) + xy + x^3 - y^3$

B. $-(2x^2y - 3xy^2 + xy) + x^3 - y^3$

C. $-2x^2y - (-3xy^2 + xy + x^3 - y^3)$

D. $-2x^2y + 3xy^2 - (xy + x^3 + y^3)$

3 $-[a - (b - c)] + d$ is equal to ( ).

A. $-a + b - c + d$

B. $-a - b + c + d$

C. $-a + b - c - d$

D. $-a + b + c + d$

B. Fill in the blanks

4 Simplify: $3a - (4a - 5b) + 2\left(\dfrac{1}{3}a - 2b\right) = $ _____.

5 Simplify: $-\left(-3x + \dfrac{2}{5}y\right) - 2\left(\dfrac{2}{3}x - y\right) = $ _____.

6 Simplify: $-[-(0.1x - y) + 2(x + 0.2y)] = $ _____.

7 Simplify: $-[-(0.1x - y)] + 2(x + 0.2y) = $ _____.

8 Half of the difference of $3x + 5y$ and $x - y$ is _____.

9 The difference of $3x + 5y$ and half of $x - y$ is _____.

10 If the value of $(ax^2 - 3x + 1) - (5 - 3x + 2x^2)$ is not related to x, then $a =$ _____.

C. Questions that require solutions

11 Given: $a^3 + b^3 = 26$ and $a^2b - ab^2 = -12$, find the value of $(a^3 - b^3) + (4ab^2 - 2a^2b) - 2(ab^2 - b^3)$.

12 In a triangle, two angles are $(x - 10)$ degrees and $(60 - 3x)$ degrees respectively. Find the measure of the remaining angle. (Note: The sum of three angles in a triangle is $180°$.)

13 Let x represent a two-digit number and y represent a one-digit number. A three-digit number M is formed with y in its ones place and the digits in the tens and ones places of x in its hundreds and tens places. Another three-digit number N is formed with y in its hundreds place and the digits in the tens and ones places of x in its tens and ones places. Explain why $M - N$ is a multiple of 9.

14 Write two algebraic expressions that satisfy the following three conditions simultaneously.

① The sum of the two algebraic expressions is $3x^2 + x - 1$.

② Both have three terms.

③ The coefficients of one of the algebraic expressions are all positive numbers, and the coefficients of the other algebraic expression are all negative numbers.

Unit test 7

A. Multiple choice questions

1 The following statement that is incorrect is (   ).

A. $\frac{1}{2}x^2$ is a monomial of degree 2.

B. $x^3 - 2xy^2 + y^3$ is an algebraic expression of degree 3 with three terms.

C. 0 is a monomial.

D. The coefficient of $-\frac{xy^2}{4}$ is -1.

2 Sam's starting salary was x pounds per month, and at the end of the first year, his salary was increased by 2.5%. His salary at the beginning of the second year is (   ) pounds per month.

A. $0.025x$ B. $x + 0.025x$

C. $x - 0.025x$ D. $x + 2.5x$

3 The value of the algebraic expression $\frac{1}{2+x}$ could not be (   ).

A. a positive number   B. a negative number

C. 0   D. 1

4 Among the following expressions, the like term of $-5ax^2$ is (   ).

A. $2ax$ B. $-3a$ C. $-5x^2$ D. $5ax^2$

5 Among the following equations, the correct one is (   ).

A. $3x^2 + 2x^3 = 5x^5$ B. $2x^2 + 3x^2 = 5x^2$

C. $2x^2 + 3x^2 = 5x^4$ D. $2x^2 + 3x^3 = 6x^5$

6 If the value of the algebraic expression $2a^2 - 3a + 1$ is 6, then the value of $4a^2 - 6a + 5$ is (   ).

A. 17   B. 15   C. 20   D. 25

B. Fill in the blanks

7 The algebraic expression representing 'the sum of 6 times the square of a and -3' is _____ .

8 Use the letters a, b and c to express the distributive law of multiplication over subtraction: _____ .

9 Use an algebraic expression to represent the difference of 3 times a squared and 4 times b cubed _____ .

10 Rearranging the algebraic expression $4x - \dfrac{2}{3}x^2 y^2 - x^3 y + 5y^3 - 7$ in descending powers of x, the result is _____ .

11 If $2x^m y^3$ and $-7xy^{2n-1}$ are like terms, then $m+n =$ _____ .

12 The opposite number of $a - b - 3x$ is _____ .

13 Simplifying $-(2m - 3n + 1.5y) - (3m + 1.5y - 3n)$, the result is _____ .

C. Questions that require solutions

14 The following flowchart shows the sequence of numerical calculation.

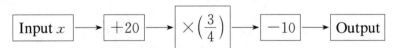

(a) Write an algebraic expression in x to express the value of the output.

(b) When the input is $x = 0$ and $x = 5$ respectively, what are the values of the output?

15 Simplify: $\frac{1}{2}a^2 - \left[\frac{1}{2}(ab - a^2) + 4ab\right] - \frac{1}{2}ab.$

16 First simplify the algebraic expression $2.3a^2 - 0.3ab + 2b^2 + 1.8ab + 1.7a^2$, then find its value for $a = \frac{1}{4}$ and $b = 16$.

17 Given $A = x^3 - 5x^2$, $B = x^2 - 11x + 6$, find the value of $A - 2B$.

18 First simplify, and then evaluate:
$$x - 2\left(\frac{1}{4}x - \frac{1}{3}y^2\right) + \left(-\frac{3}{2}x + \frac{1}{3}y^2\right), \text{ for } x = \frac{3}{2}, \ y = -2.$$

19 Choose any two-digit number, for example, 52. Swapping the digits in the number to get a new number 25 and adding them together, you get $52 + 25 = 77$. The result is a multiple of 11. Do all the two-digit numbers have the same property? Why?

20 The annual interest rate for a savings account was x %. Lisa opened an account and made an initial deposit of £5000 on 1 July 2011. She closed the account on 1 July 2016, without making any deposit or withdrawal in between. How much money should she get? Use an algebraic expression to write your answer. If the interest rate was 3.75%, how much did Lisa get at the end? (Note: Assume simple interest rate.)

21 Write two algebraic expressions that each satisfy the following three conditions simultaneously.
① The variable is x.
② It has 4 terms and a degree of 3.
③ Its value is zero for $x = 1$.

Chapter 8 Multiplying algebraic expressions

8.1 Multiplying powers with the same base (1)

Learning objective

Use the laws of indices and evaluate numerical expressions with indices

A. Multiple choice questions

1 The following calculation that is correct is (   ).

A. $a^4 \times a^4 = a^{16}$ B. $a^5 \times a^5 = a^{10}$ C. $a^6 + a^6 = a^{12}$ D. $a^7 \times a^7 = 2a^7$

2 The following calculation that is incorrect is (   ).

A. $(-a)^3 \times (-a)^3 = a^6$ B. $(-a)^2(-a)^3 = -a^5$

C. $(-a)^2 \times (-a)^4 = a^6$ D. $(-a)^3 \times (-a)^4 = a^7$

3 Calculate: the value of $\left(-\dfrac{1}{10}\right)^2 \times (-0.1)^2 \times (-1)^{100}$ is (   ).

A. -1 B. 0.1 C. -0.01 D. 0.0001

B. Fill in the blanks

4 Express the result using a single exponent [1]: $(-2)^5 \times (-2)^6 \times (-2)^7 = $ _____.

5 Express the result using a single exponent: $a \times a^2 \times a^3 \times (-a)^4 \times (-a)^5 \times (-a)^6 = $ _____.

6 Express the result using a single exponent: $a^{m+n} \times a^{2(m-n)} = $ _____.

7 Express the result using a single exponent: $(-0.125)^3 \times \left(-\dfrac{1}{8}\right)^4 = $ _____.

---

① When a number is expressed as a^b, a is called the **base**, and b is called the **exponent** (also called **power** or **index**).

8 Express the result using a single exponent: $(a+b)^5 \times (a+b) \times (a+b)^3 = $ _____.

9 Simplify: $3a^2 + 4a^2 + 5a \times 6a^4 = $ _____.

10 Simplify: $3a^2 \times 4a^2 - 5a + 6a^4 = $ _____.

C. Questions that require solutions

11 Simplify: $-a^3 \times a^6 + 2a^4 \times a^2 \times a^3 - 3a^7$.

12 Simplify: $2(a-b)^3 \times (a-b)^2 - 3(b-a)^2 \times (a-b)^3$.

13 Given: $3^m = 4$ and $3^n = 5$, find the value of 3^{m+2n}.

14 Given: $x^m = a$ and $y^n = b$, express the value of $x^{3m} \times y^{2n}$ in terms of a and b.

8.2 Multiplying powers with the same base (2)

Learning objective

Use the laws of indices and evaluate numerical expressions with indices

A. Multiple choice questions

1 Among the following expressions, the one that cannot be simplified using the rule for multiplying powers with the same base is (   ).

A. $(a+2b)(a+2b)^2$ 　　　　　　B. $(a-2b)(a+2b)^2$

C. $(a-2b)(2b-a)^3$ 　　　　　　D. $(a+2b)(2b+a)^3$

2 Among the following equations, the correct one is (   ).

A. $(-2x^2)\times x=2x^3$ 　　　　　　B. $-x^5\times(-x)^3=x^8$

C. $x^2\times x^3=x^6$ 　　　　　　D. $(x+y)^2\times(x+y)^n=(x+y)^{2n}$

3 In the equation $a^2\times(-a)\times($ $)=a^{11}$, the algebraic expression in the brackets should be (   ).

A. a^8 　　　　B. $(-a)^8$ 　　　　C. $-a^8$ 　　　　D. $(-a)^9$

B. Fill in the blanks

4 Calculate: $(-2)^{2013}+(-2)^{2014}=$ _____.

5 Calculate: $3\times2^{99}-6\times2^{98}=$ _____.

6 Simplify: $(3x)^2\times(3x)^3+(-3x)^4\times(-x)=$ _____.

7 Simplify: $(a-b)^3\times(b-a)^4-(b-a)^5\times(a-b)^2=$ _____.

8 If $a^{3n+2}\times a^{5-n}=a^n\times a^{10}$, then $n=$ _____.

9 If $2^{a+5}=9$, then $2^{a+6}=$ _____.

10 If $2^{a+5}=9$, then $3\times2^{a+4}=$ _____.

C. Questions that require solutions

11 Simplify: $\frac{1}{2}x \times xy \times x - y \times x \times x^2 + \frac{3}{2}x \times x^2 \times y$.

12 Simplify: $(y-x)^3 \times (x-y)^n + 2(x-y)^{n+1} \times (y-x)^2$.

13 An operation is defined as $a * b = 10^a \times 10^b$; for example, $2 * 1 = 10^2 \times 10^1 = 10^3$.
Calculate:
(a) $5 * 4$;

(b) $(n-2) * (5+n)$.

14 Given: $2^a = 5$, $2^b = 6$ and $2^c = 30$, write an equation involving a, b and c.

8.3 Multiplying algebraic expressions (1)

Learning objective

Multiply two algebraic expressions, including with negative coefficients and use the laws of indices

A. Multiple choice questions

1 Calculating $(-2x^4) \times (-3x^3)$, the result is (　　).

A. $6x^{12}$ B. $6x^7$ C. $-6x^{12}$ D. $-6x^7$

2 Calculating $(-2x^4)^2 \times (-3x^3)$, the result is (　　).

A. $6x^9$ B. $-6x^{11}$ C. $-12x^{11}$ D. $12x^{11}$

3 Calculating $(-2x^4)^2 \times (-3x^3)^3$, the result is (　　).

A. $-108x^{17}$ B. $108x^{17}$ C. $6x^{17}$ D. $-6x^{17}$

B. Fill in the blanks

4 Simplify: $(-5a^2 b)\left(-\dfrac{3}{5}ab^3\right) =$ _____.

5 Simplify: $(-5a^2 b)^2 \times \left(-\dfrac{3}{5}ab^3\right) =$ _____.

6 Simplify: $(-5a^n b)^2 \times (a^3 b^4)^n =$ _____.

7 Express in standard form [1]: $(4 \times 10^4) \times (5 \times 10^2) =$ _____.

8 Express in standard form: $(4.2 \times 10^5) \times (5.5 \times 10^3) =$ _____.

9 Simplify: $9(x-y)^3 \times \left[-\dfrac{1}{9}(x-y)^{m+5}\right] \times (y-x)^2 =$ _____.

---

[1] Note: when a number is expressed in standard form, $A \times 10^n$, the value of A must satisfy $1 \leqslant t < 10$.

10 $(2x^m y^n)^2 \times (\underline{\qquad})^3 = -108x^{2m+6} y^{5n+3}$.

 C. Questions that require solutions

11 Simplify: $(-5x^2 y^3)^2 \times (-2x^4 y^2)^3 \times \left(\dfrac{1}{2}xy^2\right)^4$.

12 Simplify: $\left(-\dfrac{3}{4}x^3 y^2\right)^3 \times (2xy^2)^2 - \left(-\dfrac{1}{2}x^4 y^3\right)^2 \times x^3 y^4$.

13 If $[-3(x+y)^m (x-y)^{2n}]^2 \times [-(x+y)^2] = -9(x+y)^{10}(x-y)^{12-n}$, find the values of m and n.

14 Given: $x^{2n} = 3$, find the value of $x^{4n} + (2x^n)(-5x^{5n})$.

8.4 Multiplying algebraic expressions (2)

 Learning objective

Multiply two algebraic expressions, including with negative coefficients and use the laws of indices

 A. Multiple choice questions

1. The following calculation that is correct is (　　).

   A. $(-3x^3)^2 = 9x^5$ 　　　　　B. $x(3x-2) = 3x^2 - 2x$

   C. $x^2(3x^3 - 2) = 3x^6 - 2x^2$ 　　D. $x(x^3 - x^2 + 1) = x^4 - x^3$

2. If the length, width and height of a cuboid is $5x-2$, $3x$ and $2x$ respectively, then its volume is (　　).

   A. $30x^3 - 12x^2$ 　　　　　B. $25x^3 - 10x^2$

   C. $18x^2$ 　　　　　　　　D. $10x - 2$

3. Given that $(x^{4-n} + y^{m+3}) \times x^n = x^4 + x^2 y^7$, the value of $m+n$ is (　　).

   A. 3 　　　　　　　　　　B. 4

   C. 5 　　　　　　　　　　D. 6

 B. Fill in the blanks

4. Simplify: $-4x \times \dfrac{y-x}{2} = $ _____.

5. Simplify: $15xy \times \left(-\dfrac{1}{3}x^2 yz + \dfrac{1}{5}xy^2 z\right) = $ _____.

6. Simplify: $\left(-\dfrac{4}{3}x^2 y^2\right) \times \left(\dfrac{3}{4}x^2 + xy - \dfrac{2}{5}y^2\right) = $ _____.

7. Simplify: $x^2 y \times (x^{n-1} y^{n+1} - x^{n-1} y^{n-1} + x^n y^n) = $ _____.

8. Simplify: $(x+y)^n \times [2(x+y)^{10-n} - 3(x+y)^2(x-y)^n] = $ _____.

9 If A and B are both monomials, and $5x(A-2y)=30x^2y^3+B$, then $A=$ _____ and $B=$ _____.

10 If $ab^2=-3$, then $-ab \times (a^2b^5-ab^3-b)=$ _____.

 ## C. Questions that require solutions

11 Simplify: $-2a^2\left(\dfrac{1}{2}ab+b^2\right)-5ab(a^2-ab)$, then find its value for $a=-1$ and $b=1$.

12 Solve the equation: $2x(x+1)-x(3x-2)+2x^2=x^2+1$.

13 Solve the equation: $x(x-3)=3x(x+2)-2x^2-3$.

14 Given that $(m-x)\times(-x)-(x+m)\times(-n)=5x+x^2-6$ is true for any rational number x, find the value of $m(n-1)+n(m+1)$.

8.5 Multiplying algebraic expressions (3)

Learning objective

Multiply two algebraic expressions, including with negative coefficients and use the laws of indices

A. Multiple choice questions

1 Calculating $\left(\dfrac{a}{2} - \dfrac{b}{3}\right)(3a + 2b)$, the result is (　　).

    A. $\dfrac{2}{3}a^2 - \dfrac{3}{2}b^2$　　B. $\dfrac{3}{2}a^2 - \dfrac{2}{3}b^2$　　C. $\dfrac{1}{6}(4a^2 - 9b^2)$　　D. $\dfrac{1}{6}(4a^2 + 5ab - 9b^2)$

2 Among the following calculations, the incorrect one is (　　).

    A. $(x+4)(x-5) = x^2 - x - 20$　　　　B. $(x-1)(x-6) = x^2 - 7x + 6$

    C. $(x+3)(2x-1) = 2x^2 + 5x - 3$　　　　D. $(x+1)(2x-3) = x^2 - x - 3$

3 The following calculation that has the result of $x^2 - 3x - 10$ is (　　).

    A. $(x-5)(x+2)$　　　　　　　　B. $(x+5)(x-2)$

    C. $(x-5)(x-2)$　　　　　　　　D. $(x+5)(x+2)$

B. Fill in the blanks

4 Expand and simplify: $(x+a)(x+b) = x^2 + (\underline{\hspace{2cm}})x + ab$.

5 Expand and simplify: $(ax+b)(cx+d) = (\underline{\hspace{1.5cm}})x^2 + (\underline{\hspace{1.5cm}})x + bd$.

6 Expand and simplify: $(a+3)(b-4) = \underline{\hspace{3cm}}$.

7 Expand and simplify: $(3x-2y)(2x+3y) = \underline{\hspace{3cm}}$.

8 Expand and simplify: $(3a-2b)(3a+2b) = \underline{\hspace{2cm}}$.

9 Expand and simplify: $(2a-b)(4a^2 + 2ab + b^2) = \underline{\hspace{2cm}}$.

10 If $(3x-4)(2x-1) = ax^2 + bx + c$, then $a + 2b + 3c = \underline{\hspace{2cm}}$.

C. Questions that require solutions

11 Expand and simplify:

(a) $(x+1)(x+2)(x+3)$;

(b) $(1+2x)(1-2x)(x+3)$;

(c) $(x+y-2)^2$.

12 Expand and simplify:

(a) $(a^n - b^n)^2$;

(b) $(a^n + b^n)(a^{2n} - a^n b^n + b^{2n})$.

13 Solve the equation: $(1+2x)(x+1) = (x+1)(2x+3)+10$.

14 The edge length of a cube is a cm. If the edge length is increased by 2 cm, then by how many square centimetres is the area of each face increased? By how many cubic centimetres is the volume increased?

8.6 Multiplying algebraic expressions (4)

Learning objective

Multiply two algebraic expressions, including with negative coefficients and use the laws of indices

A. Multiple choice questions

1. A three-term algebraic expression is multiplied by another three-term algebraic expression. The resulting algebraic expression before collecting like terms has (   ).

   A. 3 terms   B. 5 terms   C. 6 terms   D. 9 terms

2. Among the following expressions, the one that is equivalent to $x^2 + 10x - 24$ is (   ).

   A. $(x - 12)(x + 2)$ B. $(x + 12)(x - 2)$

   C. $(x + 4)(x + 6)$ D. $(x - 4)(x - 6)$

3. Simplifying $x(y - x) - y(x - y)$, the result is (   ).

   A. $y^2 - x^2$ B. $x^2 - y^2$ C. $2xy$ D. $-2xy$

B. Fill in the blanks

4. Expand and simplify: $\left(-\dfrac{1}{3}x^2 y\right)^2 \times (3xy^2)^3 = $ _____.

5. Expand and simplify: $-\dfrac{1}{3}x^2 y \times \left(-\dfrac{1}{3}x^2 y + 3xy^2\right) = $ _____.

6. Expand and simplify: $(x + 2y^2)(x - 2y^2) = $ _____.

7. Expand and simplify: $(a + 2b)^2 - (a - 2b)^2 = $ _____.

8. Expand and simplify: $(a - b)(a + b)(a^2 + b^2) = $ _____.

9. Expand and simplify: $(1 + a^2)(1 - a^2 + a^4) = $ _____.

10. If $(x - 3) \times A = x^2 + 2x - 15$, then $A = $ _____.

C. Questions that require solutions

11 Expand and simplify:

(a) $(a-2b+3)(a+2b-3)$;

(b) $(a+2)(a+3)(a+4)$.

12 Solve the equation: $(x+3)^2+(x+2)(x-1)=(x-3)(2x+1)-2$.

13 Given that the product of $(x^2+ax+3)(x^2-3x+b)$ contains neither x^2 nor the constant term, find the values of a and b.

14 Alvin and Joe calculated $(3x+a)(4x+b)$ respectively. Alvin made a mistake about the sign of a and obtained his result as $12x^2+17x+6$. Joe mistook $4x$ as x and obtained his result as $3x^2+7x-6$. Answer the following.

(a) What are the values of a and b ?

(b) What is the correct result of the calculation?

Unit test 8

A. Multiple choice questions

1. Among the following calculations, the correct one is (   ).

    A. $a \times a^5 = a^5$ B. $a^2 \times a^3 = a^6$ C. $a^2 + a^3 = a^5$ D. $a^3 \times a^7 = a^{10}$

2. In the equation $x^2 \cdot (-x)^3 \cdot ($ $) = x^{10}$, the algebraic expression in the brackets should be (   ).

    A. x^2 B. $(-x)^2$ C. x^5 D. $(-x)^5$

3. A two-term algebraic expression is multiplied by a three-term algebraic expression. The resulting algebraic expression before collecting like terms has (   ).

    A. 2 terms   B. 3 terms   C. 5 terms   D. 6 terms

4. If the length and width of a rectangle are $3x + 5$ and $2x$, then its area is (   ).

    A. $6x^2 + 10$ B. $6x^2 + 10x$ C. $5x^2 + 7x$ D. $10x + 10$

5. If $(a+5) \times M = a^2 + 3a - 10$, then $M = ($ $)$.

    A. $a + 2$ B. $a - 2$ C. $a + 2$ D. $2a - 5$

B. Fill in the blanks

6. Express the result using a single exponent: $(-3)^8 \times (-3)^{10} \times (-3)^{15} = $ _____ .

7. Express the result using a single exponent: $a \times (-a)^{10} \times a^{100} \times (-a)^{1000} = $ _____ .

8. If $x^{a+3} = 100$, then $x^{a+4} = $ _____ and $x^{2a+6} = $ _____ .

9. Calculate: $(-3)^{2016} + (-3)^{2017} = -2 \times ($ _____ $)^{(\ \ )}$.

10. Calculate: given $y^m = 10$ and $y^n = 13$, then $y^{3m+n} = $ _____ .

⑪ Expand and simplify: $(2x)^3 \times (-3x^2 y^3) = $ _____.

⑫ Expand and simplify: $(x-a)(x-b) = x^2 - ($ _____$)x + $ _____.

⑬ Expand and simplify: $(2a+b)(a+2b) = $ _____.

⑭ Expand and simplify: $(-x+y)(5x-y) = $ _____.

⑮ Expand and simplify: $(2m+3n)(3n-m) = $ _____.

C. Questions that require solutions

⑯ Given: $x^m = 3p$ and $y^n = 2q$, express the value of $x^{2m} \times y^{3n}$ in terms of p and q.

⑰ If $m+n = 8$ and $mn = 12$, find the value of $mn^2 + m^2 n$.

⑱ Expand and simplify: $(2x+y)^2 - (2x+3y)(2x-3y)$, then find its value for $x = 2$ and $y = 3$.

19 Amy, Joy and Evan work in a large company. Joy's salary is £200 more than Amy's salary, and Evan's salary is £80 less than twice Joy's salary.

(a) If Amy's monthly salary is x pounds, express these three people's total monthly salary in terms of x and simplify.

(b) If Amy's monthly salary is £2300, how much is their total monthly salary?

20 The diagram shows a rectangular piece of paper, $a = 12$ cm and $b = 6$ cm. A square with side length x is cut from each corner. If the total area of the parts cut off is equal to that of the remaining part, what is the side length of the square cut off from each corner?

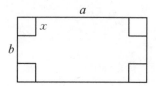

Diagram for question 20

Chapter 9 Events and possibilities[*]

9.1 Introduction to possibility

 Learning objective

Use and understand the language associated with probability

 A. Multiple choice questions

1 If the weather forecast says there is a 90% chance of rain tomorrow, then the correct statement is (   ).

A. It must rain tomorrow.

B. There will definitely be no rain tomorrow.

C. There is a high chance of rain tomorrow.

D. The forecast is not really meaningful.

2 Jim is asked to choose any number from 1 to 10. The incorrect statement is (   ).

A. It is possible that the number he chooses is divisible by 2.

B. It is possible that the number he chooses is divisible by 3.

C. It is possible that the number he chooses is divisible by 7.

D. It is possible that the number he chooses is divisible by both 2 and 7.

 B. Fill in the blanks

3 Choose 'definitely', 'possibly' or 'impossible' to fill in the following blanks.

In general, to describe the possibility of something, when it is certain that it will happen, we use the term _____ ; when it is certain that it will not happen, we say _____ ; and when it is uncertain whether it will or will not happen, we say _____ .

---

[*] This chapter is also a preparation for learning of probability.

4 There are two boxes, each of which contains 4 identical blocks. Box A contains 4 red blocks and Box B contains 2 red blocks and 2 yellow blocks. Joan picks a block from one of the boxes.

(a) From Box _____ , Joan will definitely get a red block.

(b) From Box _____ , Joan will definitely not get a yellow block.

(c) From Box _____ , Joan will possibly get a yellow block.

5 Which of the following events will definitely happen (put a √)? Which of them are impossible (put a ✗)? Which may possibly happen (put a △)?

(a) The index of the London Stock Exchange on the next trading day goes up.

                                                                                 (   )

(b) Everyone's age increases year by year. (   )

(c) The Earth moves around the Moon. (   )

(d) Mary scores higher in the next test than the last test. (   )

(e) New babies are born every day in the world. (   )

(f) There are 15 months in a year. (   )

(g) Summer follows after spring. (   )

(h) A chicken lays eggs. (   )

(i) Tom can run 1000 metres in less than 1 minute. (   )

(j) The hour hand of a clock moves 24 rounds every day. (   )

C. Questions that require solutions

6 Colour the cubes in the boxes as indicated.

(a) A cube taken out of the box is definitely a blue cube.

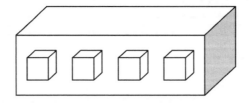

(b) A cube taken out of the box is definitely not a blue cube.

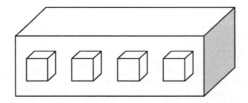

(c) A cube taken out of the box is possibly a blue cube.

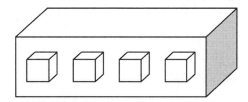

7 The diagram shows four blocks in each of the three boxes. A block is taken out of these boxes. Answer the following questions.

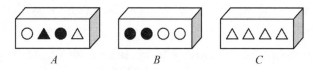

(a) From which box will the block taken out definitely be a △?

(b) From which box is it impossible to pick out a ● ?

(c) From which box is it possible to pick out a ○?

(d) From which box is it impossible to pick out a ▲?

9.2 Comparing possibilities: how likely is it?

Learning objective

Describe events and their possibilities as fractions and percentages

A. Multiple choice questions

1. A bag contains some identical square cards, each of which is numbered. Three cards are numbered 1, five cards are numbered 2, four cards are numbered 3 and one card is numbered 4. A card is to be taken out of the bag.

   (a) It is most likely that the card taken out will be numbered (   ).

       A. 1   B. 2   C. 3   D. 4

   (b) It is least likely that the card taken out will be numbered (   ).

       A. 1   B. 2   C. 3   D. 4

2. Considering the conditions given in question 1, the incorrect statement is (   ).

   A. It is more likely that the card will have a number greater than 2 than a number less than 2.

   B. It is more likely that the card will have an odd number than an even number.

   C. It is more likely that the card will have a number that is a multiple of 3 than a multiple of 2.

   D. All of the above are incorrect.

B. Fill in the blanks

3. The weather forecast predicted a 30% chance of rain on one day in London and a 60% chance of rain in Manchester. It was _____ likely that there was rain in Manchester than in London on the day. (Choose 'more' or 'less' to fill in.)

4. The chance of winning a lottery prize is 7%. Tom's father bought a lottery ticket. He is _____ likely to win a prize than not win a prize. (Choose 'more' or 'less' to fill in.)

5. Mr Wood bought some gifts for his class: 8 pencil cases, 15 notebooks and 12 science books. Each pupil is given a chance to receive one gift by drawing lots. If

Tom is the first pupil to draw lots, the gift he is most likely to receive is _____ , and the gift he is least likely to receive is _____ .

C. Questions that require solutions

6 Colour the divided sections of the spinning wheel so that when it spins, the pointer is more likely to land on the red section than the yellow section.

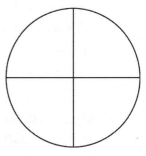

Diagram for question 6

7 Colour the divided sections of the spinning wheel so that when it spins, the pointer is most likely to land on the red section and least likely to land on the green section, while the possibility that the pointer will land on the yellow section is the same as it is to land on the blue section.

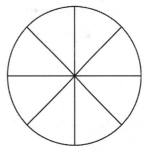

Diagram for question 7

8 A bag contains 5 identical balls each marked with 1, 2, 3, 4 and 5 respectively. Joan and Matt take turns to pick a ball from the bag and then put it back. The rule is that if the number marked on the ball Joan picked is greater than 3, then she wins; otherwise Matt wins. Do you think that it is a fair game? If it is not, how can you change the rule so it becomes a fair game?

9 There are 54 cards in a set of playing cards, including the two Jokers. Kath and Lin are playing a game of drawing cards.

(a) Compared with the possibility of Lin drawing a diamond, what is the possibility of Kath drawing a club?

(b) Compared with the possibility of Lin drawing a Joker, what is the possibility of Kath drawing an 'Ace'?

(c) Compared with the possibility of Lin drawing a card that is less than 9, what is the possibility of Kath drawing a card that is greater than 9?

10 If a number is drawn randomly from consecutive integers from 50 to 150, identify what number of the following is more likely to come up:

(a) a two-digit number or a three-digit number;

(b) a multiple of 3 or a multiple of 5.

9.3 Working out possibilities (1)

Learning objective

Explore all possible outcomes and solve related problems

A. Multiple choice questions

1. A box contains one blue ball, one yellow ball and one red ball. Pat picks a ball from the bag. Its possible outcome is (   ).
   A. a blue ball   B. a yellow ball   C. a red ball   D. all of the above

2. There are (   ) possible outcomes if a number is chosen from integers 1 to 6.
   A. 3   B. 4   C. 5   D. 6

3. There are (   ) possible outcomes if an even number is chosen from integers 1 to 6.
   A. 3   B. 4   C. 5   D. 6

B. Fill in the blanks

4. Sam is asked by her teacher to choose any multiple of 4 from integers 10 to 20. There are _____ possible outcomes of the number Sam will choose and they are _____ .

5. In a student celebration party, the organisers prepared four types of fruit for students. They are oranges, bananas, pears and apples.
   (a) If each student can choose any, but only one, type of fruit, he or she has _____ choices.
   (b) If each student can choose any two types of fruit, he or she has _____ choices.
   (c) If each student can choose any two pieces of fruit from the same type or different types, he or she has _____ choices.

C. Questions that require solutions

6 Draw any two cards consecutively from the four cards $\boxed{1}$ $\boxed{2}$ $\boxed{3}$ $\boxed{4}$ to form a two-digit number.

(a) How many different two-digit numbers can possibly be formed?

(b) How many possibilities are there for the sums of the two numbers on the cards?

(c) Among the two-digit numbers formed, how many are there whose digits add up to 5?

(d) Among the two-digit numbers formed, how many are multiples of 3?

(e) Among the two-digit numbers formed, how many numbers are greater than 12?

7 A teacher puts students into groups of four for an event. One group consists of Tom, Mary, Joseph and Ian, and they need to select a group leader.

(a) If any one of them can serve as the group leader, how many possibilities are there? List all of them.

(b) If any two of them can serve as the group leader and the assistant group leader respectively, how many possibilties are there? List all of them.

8 Draw three cards consecutively from the four cards ①②③④ to form a three-digit number.

(a) How many different three-digit numbers can possibly be formed?

(b) How many possibilities are there for the sums of the three numbers on the cards?

(c) Among the three-digit numbers formed, how many are multiples of 5?

(d) Among the three-digit numbers formed, how many are less than 324?

(e) What is the sum of all the three-digit numbers formed?

9.4 Working out possibilities (2)

Learning objective

Explore all possible outcomes and solve related problems

A. Multiple choice questions

1. Using three cards marked with 0, 5 and 9, we can possibly form _____ three-digit numbers.

    A. 2   B. 4   C. 6   D. 9

2. A basketball tournament has five teams A, B, C, D and E. The two teams that will play the first game will be decided by drawing lots. There are _____ different possibilities of the two teams that will play the first game.

    A. 5   B. 10

    C. 20   D. none of the above

B. Fill in the blanks

3. Draw three cards from the four cards ⓪ ① ② ③ to form a three-digit number.

    (a) _____ three-digit numbers can be formed.

    (b) _____ three-digit numbers without 0 as one of its digits can be formed.

    (c) _____ three-digit even numbers can be formed.

4. Team A has 6 members, Team B has 8 members and Team C has 9 members. One member from each team is selected to attend a meeting. In total, there are _____ different selections of the attendees from the three teams.

C. Questions that require solutions

5. A black dice and a white dice are thrown at the same time. Considering the two numbers the dice land on, answer the following questions.

    (a) How many possible results are there?

    (b) Among all the possible results, how many are there whose sums are multiples of 2?

244

(c) Among all the possible results, how many are there whose differences are not less than 2?

(Note: a dice has six faces labelled 1 to 6. You may use a tree diagram or make a table to find the answers.)

6 Two girls and three boys are to form a row for a photo.
(a) How many different ways of standing are there in total?

(b) If the two girls need to stand side by side, then how many different ways of standing are there in total?

(c) If the three boys need to stand side by side, then how many different ways of standing are there in total?

7 The diagram shows a 16-square grid. Put 4 counters, which are red, white, blue and black respectively, in the square cells, so there is one counter for each row and one counter for each column. How many different ways are there to put the counters on the grid?

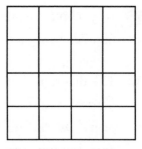

Diagram for question 7

9.5　Events of equal possibility

Solve problems involving events of equal possibilities

 A. Multiple choice questions

1　An opaque bag contains three identical balls in three different colours: red, yellow and green. If a ball is randomly taken out of the bag, then it is (　　).
　A. a red ball　　　　　　　　　　　B. a yellow ball
　C. a green ball　　　　　　　　　　D. all of the above are possible

2　Randomly pick one card from a deck of 52 playing cards, excluding the two Jokers. The possibility of picking an 'Ace' is (　　).

　A. $\dfrac{1}{52}$　　　　B. $\dfrac{1}{4}$　　　　C. $\dfrac{1}{13}$　　　　D. 1

3　30 cards are numbered from 1 to 30. First remove the cards whose numbers are multiples of 3 and then remove the remaining cards whose numbers are multiples of 2. If the remaining cards are put in order from the least to the greatest, then the number on the fifth card is (　　).
　A. 7　　　　　　B. 11　　　　　　C. 13　　　　　　D. 17

B. Fill in the blanks

4　When a dice is thrown, the possibility of it landing on a number greater than 4 is _____ .

5　If you pick a number randomly from integers 1 to 20, the possibility of the number being a prime number is _____ .

6　The diagram shows six wooden squares, each labelled with a number. All the squares are the same size and can be flipped over. On the backs of the six squares, only two of them have the winning sign. If you flip one square randomly, the possibility of it showing the winning sign is _____ .

| 1 | 2 | 3 |
| 4 | 5 | 6 |

Diagram for question 6

7 Allen, Nick and James are passing a ball to each other. Each person can pass it freely to either of the other two people. James starts passing the ball. After the ball is passed 3 times, the possibility of the ball going back to James on the third pass is _____ .

8 An opaque bag contains 4 red balls, 5 yellow balls and 1 white ball. Jack first took out a yellow ball from the bag and then put it back. He then took out another ball from the bag. The possibility of him taking out a yellow ball the second time is _____ . (Fill in with a fraction.)

C. Questions that require solutions

9 Kevin designed a target board as shown in the diagram. He divided the four circles, which have the same centre, into 6 equal parts using grey and white colours. If a dart is randomly thrown at the target, what is the possibility of hitting a white part?

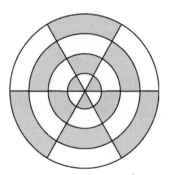

Diagram for question 9

10 A dice is rolled once. What is the possibility of the following outcome?
(a) The number landed on is 2.
(b) The number landed on is a multiple of 3.
(c) The number landed on is an odd number.

11 When three people with different heights are standing in a row from left to right, what is the possibility of them standing from the shortest to the tallest, starting from the left?

12 Ling is throwing a fair dice to study the outcomes of the numbers landed on.

(a) If he throws the dice once, what is the possibility of him landing on a prime number?

(b) If he throws the dice twice and uses the two numbers landed on to form a two-digit number, so the first outcome is in the tens place and the second outcome is in the ones place, then what is the possibility that the two-digit number is a prime number?

(c) If he throws the dice three times, and uses the first, second and third outcome as the digit in the hundreds, tens and ones places respectively to form a three-digit number, then what is the possibility that the three-digit number is a multiple of 5?

Unit test 9

A. Fill in the blanks

1 A bag contains 3 red blocks, 2 white blocks, 3 yellow blocks and 5 green blocks. If a block is taken out of the bag, it is most likely to be a _____ block and least likely to be a _____ block.

2 Fill in the blanks with 'definitely', 'possible' (possibly) or 'impossible'.
   (a) It is raining today. It will _____ rain again tomorrow.
   (b) The elder sister is _____ older than her younger sister.
   (c) It is _____ for the Sun to rise from the west.
   (d) It is _____ that Tom will win a prize in the maths competition.
   (e) It is _____ for both teams to score 1000 in a basketball match.

3 There are three boxes labelled A, B and C, each containing several identical balls in various colours. Box A contains 4 white balls, Box B contains 2 red balls and 2 white balls, and Box C contains 4 black balls. Maria is asked to pick a ball from one of the boxes.
   (a) If the ball is picked from Box _____, it is definitely a white ball.
   (b) If the ball is picked from Box _____, it is definitely a black ball.
   (c) If the ball is picked from Box _____, it is possible to be a red ball.
   (d) If the ball is picked from Box _____, it is impossible to be a white ball.

4 Belle and Lily are playing with some dice. They throw 2 dice together each time. Belle says: 'I will win if the sum of the two numbers I land on is an even number and you will win if the sum of the two numbers is an odd number.' If this is the rule, then _____ is more likely to win.

5 There are two 5p coins, one 50p coin and two 10p coins. Choose any two coins and add their values. It is _____ likely that the total value is an even number. (Fill in with 'more' or 'less'.)

6 Fay has 4 shirts, 3 pairs of trousers and 2 pairs of shoes. She can have _____ days wearing different combinations of her clothing.

7 A football tournament has 8 teams. The two teams that will play the first game will be decided by drawing lots. There are _____ different combinations of the two teams playing the first game.

8 If a coin is tossed and a dice is rolled at the same time, the possibility of getting both the head facing up on the coin and a number greater than 4 on the dice is _____ .

B. Multiple choice questions

9 Choose any two cards from the four cards marked with 9, 8, 7 and 6. The product of the two numbers on the cards is most likely to be _____ .
A. an odd number
B. an even number
C. a single-digit number
D. less than 50

10 There are _____ combinations of three-digit numbers with the three cards marked with 4, 5 and 6.
A. 8   B. 6   C. 3   D. 1

11 A box contains 2 white cards, 3 black cards and 4 red cards. All of them are indentical in terms of their size and shape. 8 cards are now drawn from the box. Will the cards have all the three colours? The answer is _____ .
A. yes, definitely
B. yes, it is possible
C. no, it is impossible
D. not sure

12 The weather forecast says: 'There is 70% chance of rain tomorrow.' Based on this forecast, the correct statement is (   ).
A. It will definitely rain tomorrow.
B. It is impossible to rain tomorrow.
C. It is more likely to rain tomorrow.
D. It is equally likely to rain or not to rain tomorrow.

13 The correct statement is (   ).
A. 'Unlikely' means 'impossible'.

B. Saying 'something will definitely happen' or 'it is impossible that something will happen' means it is certain whether something will happen or not.

C. Saying 'something will most likely happen' means it will definitely happen.

D. Saying 'two things may possibly happen' means they are equally likely to happen.

14 Link each statement about possibility on the right with the correct condition(s) on the left.

What balls are in the box?

A. 4 black balls

B. 3 white balls and 1 black ball

C. 3 black balls and 1 white ball

D. 3 red balls and 1 white ball

E. 4 white balls

What is the possibilility that a ball taken from the box will be a particular colour?

(1) It is definitely a white ball.

(2) It is impossible for it to be a black ball.

(3) The possibility of picking a white ball is $\frac{3}{4}$.

(4) The possibility of picking a black ball is $\frac{3}{4}$.

(5) It is possible for it to be a red ball.

C. Questions that require solutions

15 Dawn and Lucy are playing number cards. There are in total 9 cards numbered 1 to 9. If the card picked is greater than 5, then Dawn wins. If it is not greater than 5, Lucy wins.

(a) Do you think that the rule of the game is fair? Explain why.

(b) To make it fair, how should the rule be amended?

16 A bag contains 8 balls of identical size: 1 red ball, 3 yellow balls and 4 blue balls. Take a ball randomly from the bag.

(a) What colour ball is least likely to be picked?

(b) What colour ball has the possibility of $\frac{1}{2}$ of being picked?

(c) What is the possibility of a yellow ball being picked?

17 4 yellow and 6 white table tennis balls are put into a schoolbag. You are given a chance to take a ball randomly from the schoolbag.

(a) What colour table tennis ball are you more likely to pick?

(b) How many ways can you change your balls with only 2 balls so there is equal possibility for a yellow ball and a white ball to be picked?

18 There are 5 cards on the table marked 1, 2, 3, 4 and 5 respectively. How many different two-digit numbers can be formed? Is the two-digit number formed more likely to be a multiple of 4 or a multiple of 5?

19 There are two groups of numbers. Group A consists of 1, 3, 5, 7 and 9, and
Group B consists of 2, 4, 6, 8 and 10.

   (a) Pick a number from each group and add them up. Is the sum more likely to be
   an odd number or an even number?

   (b) How many different sums are there in the above question (a)?

   (c) Pick a number from each group and multiply. Is the product more likely to be
   an odd number or an even number?

   (d) What is the possibility of the product being a multiple of 5 in question (c)?

20 Randomly pick a number from integers 10 to 30.

   (a) What is the possibility of getting a prime number?

   (b) What is the possibility of getting a multiple of 3?

End of year test

A. Multiple choice questions (30%)

1. If $0 < a < b < 1$, then the quotient of $a \div b$ must be (   ).

   A. < 0 B. $< a$

   C. $> a$ D. all the above answers are possible

2. Among the following equations, the one from which you can get $a < 1$ is (   ).

   A. $a \div 0.1 = 1$ B. $a \times 0.8 = 1$

   C. $6.3 \div a = 1$ D. $0.8 \times a = 1$

3. In the four numbers 0.707, $0.7\overset{\cdot}{0}\overset{\cdot}{7}$, $0.\overset{\cdot}{7}0\overset{\cdot}{7}$ and $0.70\overset{\cdot}{7}$, the greatest number is (   ).

   A. 0.707 B. $0.7\overset{\cdot}{0}\overset{\cdot}{7}$ C. $0.\overset{\cdot}{7}0\overset{\cdot}{7}$ D. $0.70\overset{\cdot}{7}$

4. $5 \div \dfrac{1}{5} + 3 \times \dfrac{1}{3}$ is equal to (   ).

   A. 2 B. $\dfrac{28}{3}$ C. 26 D. 34

5. There are two numbers. One is 420. It is 10 less than 10 times the other number. The other number is (   ).

   A. $420 \times 10 - 10$ B. $420 \times 10 + 10$

   C. $(420 - 10) \div 10$ D. $(420 + 10) \div 10$

6. There are 135 peach trees in an orchard, which is 15 more than twice the number of pear trees. The number of apple trees is 3 fewer than twice the number of pear trees.

   To find how many pear trees there are in the orchard, the number sentence is (   ).

   To find how many apple trees there are in the orchard, the number sentence is (   ).

   A. $135 \times 2 + 15$ B. $(135 - 15) \div 2$

   C. $(135 - 15) \div 2 \times 2 - 3$ D. $(135 + 15) \div 2 \times 2 - 3$

7 10 is (　　) of 50 and 100.

    A. the lowest common multiple   B. a common multiple

    C. the highest common factor   D. a common factor

8 The lowest common multiple of 24 and 36 is (　　).

    A. 1   B. 12   C. 72   D. 144

9 In the algebraic expression $3a - 4x^5 - 2a^3 x^3$, the coefficient of the term with the highest degree is (　　).

    A. 5   B. 6   C. -4 D. -2

10 If the difference of an algebraic expression and $2a^2 + 4ab - 3b^2$ is $3a^2 - 2ab - b^2$, then the algebraic expression is (　　).

    A. $a^2 - 6ab + 2b^2$ B. $5a^2 + 6ab - 4b^2$

    C. $5a^2 + 2ab - 4b^2$ D. $-a^2 + 6ab - 2b^2$

11 The shaded part in the diagram shows a petal graph by connecting parts of the circumferences of small circles. The black points are the centres of these circles. The radius of each circle is 1. The area of the petal graph is (　　).

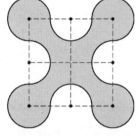

    A. 16   B. $16 + \pi$

    C. $16 + \dfrac{1}{2}\pi$ D. $16 + 2\pi$

Diagram for question 11

12 Among the following statements, the incorrect one is (　　).

    A. A box contains 8 red balls, 6 green balls and 4 white balls. Randomly picking a ball from the box, the possibility of getting a green ball is $\dfrac{1}{3}$.

    B. When throwing a dice, the possibility of getting an even number is $\dfrac{1}{3}$.

    C. Randomly picking a card from a deck of 54 playing cards (including the two Jokers), the possibility of getting a number 10 is $\dfrac{2}{27}$.

    D. There are 2 defective sets in a batch of 100 TV sets. Randomly selecting one TV set from that batch for inspection, the possibility of getting a defective set is $\dfrac{1}{50}$.

13 Two identical cubes with edge length 6 cm are put together to form a cuboid. The surface area of the cuboid is ( ).

    A. 72 cm²   B. 360 cm²   C. 396 cm²   D. 432 cm²

14 The diagram shows square $ABCD$. Point O lies on AC, and $OA = \frac{1}{4}AC$. If square $ABCD$ is rotated around point O so its image coincides with its original position, then the rotation is at least for ( ).

    A. 45°   B. 90°

    C. 180°   D. 360°

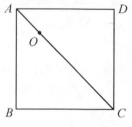

Diagram for question 14

15 The diagram shows the locations of A and B and $\angle BAC = 150°$. The correct statement of the following is ( ).

    A. A is in the direction 60° east of north from B.

    B. A is in the direction 30° east of north from B.

    C. B is in the direction 60° east of north from A.

    D. B is in the direction 30° east of north from A.

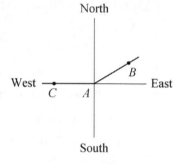

Diagram for question 15

B. Fill in the blanks (30%)

16 A pair of leather shoes was sold for £240 with a profit of 20%. To get a profit of 30%, the price of the shoes should be increased to £_____.

17 Given that the diameter of a circular flowerbed is 2 m, the circumference of the flowerbed is about _____ m.

18 The population of the United Kingdom in 2016 is estimated to be 65 348 000, which can be written in standard form as _____.

19 Given that A, B and C are on the same line, $AB = 15$ cm and $BC = 12$ cm, then the length of the line segment AC is _____ cm.

20 If City A is in the direction 40° east of north from City B, then City B is in the direction _____ from City A.

21 In a cuboid, the difference of the sum of the number of faces and number of vertices subtracted by the number of the edges is _____.

22 The diagram shows point O on line AB, $\angle AOD = 120°$, $CO \perp AB$ at point O, and OE bisects $\angle BOD$. There are _____ pairs of supplementary angles in the diagram.

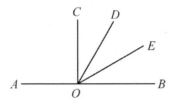

Diagram for question 22

23 The diagram shows cuboid $ABCD - EFGH$. The edge(s) that is/are neither intersecting nor parallel to edges AB and AE is/are _____.

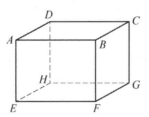

Diagram for question 23

24 Simplify: $(-x^2) \times (-x)^2 = $ _____.

25 Expand and simplify: $(x-2)(x+3) = $ _____.

26 There are two £1 coins, three 50p coins and two 10p coins. If you pick any two coins and add them up, there are _____ different values.

27 There are six balls in a bag: ○○○○○●. George picks up one ball and then puts it back. If each time he gets a white ball for the first five times, he will _____ pick up a black ball the sixth time. (Choose 'definitely' or 'possibly' or 'definitely not' to fill in.)

28 As shown in the diagram, translating △*ABC* 1 cm in the direction of *BC* gives △*DEF*. If △*ABC* has a perimeter of 8 cm, the perimeter of quadrilateral *ABFD* is _____ cm.

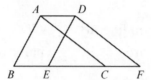

Diagram for question 28

29 As shown in the diagram, flipping △*ABC* over line *DE* gives △*A′DE*. If ∠*A′EC* = 32°, then ∠*A′ED* = _____ .

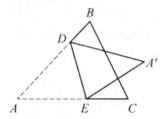

Diagram for question 29

30 In the diagram, the dots are arranged in the following pattern: counting outwards, the first loop from the inside has four dots, and the second loop has eight dots, and so on. Letting the number of dots in the *n*th loop be *y*, use an algebraic expression in *n* to represent *y*. *y* = _____ .

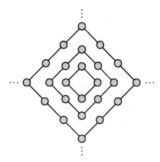

Diagram for question 30

C. Short answer questions (16%)

31 Calculate: $1.8 \div \dfrac{6}{7} \times \dfrac{5}{21}$.

32 Find the lowest common multiple and highest common factor of 24 and 60.

33 Expand and simplify: $4x - 2(3 - 2x + x^2) + 3(2x^2 - 3)$.

34 Solve the equation: $\dfrac{2x+1}{3} + 5 = \dfrac{x-7}{2}$.

D. Questions that require solutions (24%)

35 Randomly pick any two numbers from 0, 1, 2 and 3 to form a two-digit number.

(a) Write all the possible two-digit numbers that can be formed.

(b) Is it more likely that the two-digit number formed is an odd number or an even number?

(c) What is the possibility of getting a number that is a multiple of 5?

36 Given $AB = a$ and $MN = b$,

    (a) ① Construct a point C on segment AB, so that $AC = a - b$.

      ② Construct the midpoint D of AC and the midpoint E of BC.

    (b) If $a = 20$, then the segment $DE = $ _____.

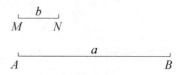

Diagram for question 36

37 Alvin wants to deposit £1000 into a savings account.

    (a) If the annual interest rate is 2.2% and he keeps the money in the account for one year, how much interest can he get at the end of the year when the deposit is mature? (Ignore the interest tax.)

    (b) If the annual interest rate is 2.2% and he keeps the money in the account for two years but needs to pay 20% on the interest earned, how much will he actually get including the principle and the interest when the deposit is mature?

38 A man travels 8 km more per hour by cycling than by walking. If the time he takes to travel 12 km by walking is the same as the time he takes to travel 36 km by cycling, find his cycling speed.

39 (a) Draw triangle $A_1B_1C_1$ that is obtained by translating triangle ABC 6 units right and then 1 unit down.

(b) After the triangle ABC is rotated 180 degrees around a certain point, the image of point B is point B_2. Draw the image, triangle $A_2B_2C_2$, of the triangle ABC after the 180 degree rotation.

(c) Through certain transformations, the triangle $A_2B_2C_2$ drawn in (b) can be also obtained from triangle $A_1B_1C_1$ drawn in (a). Write down one such transformation.

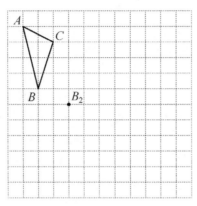

Diagram for question 39

40 The diagram shows a circular running track. The outer circumference is 31.4 m and the width of the track is 2 m.

(a) What is the area of the running track?

(b) The running track needs to be paved with sand. If each square metre of the track needs to be paved with 0.5 tons of sand, how many tons of sand are needed for the whole running track?

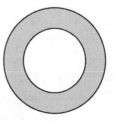

Diagram for question 40

Answers

Chapter 1 Working with numbers

1.1 Four operations with whole numbers: revision (1)

1 B **2** D **3** C **4** C **5** (a) $<$
(b) $=$ (c) $>$ (d) $=$ (e) $<$ (f) $<$
6 (b) 444 444 (c) 6800 (d) 3300
7 (a) 4430 (b) 1 000 000 (c) 19 000
(d) 11 979 (e) 288 (f) 600 **8** (a) 11 106
(b) 332 667 (c) $2006 \times 10\,001 \times 2005 - 2006 \times 2005 \times 10\,001 = 0$

1.2 Four operations with whole numbers: revision (2)

1 A **2** B **3** A, B, C and D
4 (b) $213 + (1001 + 999)$ $213 + 2000$ 2213
(c) $125 \times 80 + 125 \times 8$ $10\,000 + 1000$ 11 000
(d) $(6000 \times 8) \div (125 \times 8)$ $48\,000 \div 1000$ 48
5 (a) 2 (b) 15 (c) 12 (d) 7 (e) 6
(f) 100 **6** (a) 11 000 (b) 160
7 (a) 1 100 000 (b) 704 **8** 64 (hours)
9 12 (pages)

1.3 Working with decimals and fractions: revision (3)

1 D **2** D **3** B **4** C **5** tens
hundredths **6** 13. 303 m $>$ 13. 3 m $>$ 130. 03 cm
$>$ 13. 33 cm $>$ 13. 03 cm **7** 14 **8** 11.27
9 (a) 43.93 (b) 4030 (c) 100 (d) 1
(e) 0 (f) 1000 (g) 0.51 (h) 10.73
10 (a) 37.3 (b) 48.55 (c) 25.38 (d) 24
11 $134.6 - 33.2 = 101.4$(kg); $300 - 134.6 - (134.6 - 33.2) = 64$(kg) **12** $53.60 \div 10 = 5.36$ (pounds); $5.36 \times 100 = 536$ (pounds)
13 22.76 cm **14** (a) $(0.96 + 1.58 + 1.61 + 1.36) \div 4 = 1.3775$(m) ≈ 1.38(m) (b) $38\frac{3}{10} \times 4 = 153\frac{1}{5}$(kg) or 153. 2(kg)

1.4 Factors, common factors and highest common factors

1 B **2** D **3** C **4** C **5** C
6 $2 \times 3 \times 5$ unique **7** 1, 2 and 4, 2, 4
8 1 1 **9** A, 7 **10** 10 **11** 5 **12** (b) 1
(c) 8 (d) 17 **13** (b) 12 (c) 5 (d) 14
14 6 cm, 40 **15** 44 streetlights [Hint: $1625 = 25 \times 65$, $1170 = 18 \times 65$, and $(25, 18) = 1$, so $(1625, 1170) = 65$, $25 + 18 + 1 = 44$]

1.5 Multiples, common multiples and lowest common multiples

1 B **2** C **3** B **4** infinitely many, the least common multiple **5** 4, 48 **6** $A \times B$, 55 **7** B, 18 **8** 84, 14 **9** (b) 40
(c) 51 (d) 126 **10** (b) 16 (c) 360
11 48 students (Hint: $[8, 12] = 24$, $24 \times 2 = 48$) **12** 26 marks (Hint: $[10, 12] = 60$, $1500 \div 60 + 1 = 26$)

1.6 Multiplying two decimal numbers (1)

1 D **2** D **3** C **4** A. 18 B. 1.8
C. 0.018 D. 0.18 **5** 100, 100, 472. 44;
one, one, 472. 44, two **6** 17 **7** (a) 7.83
(b) 6.205 (c) 142.83 (d) 8.484
8 (a) 298. 3 (km) (b) $0.3 \times 0.3 = 0.09$
(m²), $0.09 \times 180 = 16.2$ (m²), 16.2 m² $>$
15. 2 m², yes. (c) £54.49

1.7 Multiplying two decimal numbers (2)

1 B **2** C **3** A **4** C **5** D
6 (a) 14.84 (b) 1.61 (c) 0.0336
7 7.2, 4.8, 0.72, 0.072 **8** (a) $>$
(b) $<$ (c) $<$ (d) $>$ **9** 131.2, 131.2,
1.312, 13 120, 1.312, 0.1312 **10** $19.5 = 7.5 \times 2.6 = 0.75 \times 26 = 75 \times 0.26$, or $1.95 = 7.5 \times 0.26 = 0.75 \times 2.6 = 75 \times 0.026$ (answer may vary) **11** (a) 0.448 (b) 10.7304
(c) 0.1494 (d) 0.04832 **12** 178.125(km)

1.8 Division by a decimal number (1)

1 B **2** B **3** C **4** (D), (B), (A)
5 5, 50, 18.2 **6** (b) 0.1 (c) 0.8
(d) 12.5 (e) 1.8 (f) 0.032 **7** (a) 16
(pieces) (b) 124 800(sets) (c) 75.6(km/h)
(d) 8.9(litres)

1.9 Division by a decimal number (2)

1 D **2** A **3** C **4** 80, 8, 1.2, 0.8,
0.08 **5** (a) $<$ (b) $>$ (c) $>$ (d) $>$
(e) $<$ (f) $=$ (g) $>$ (h) $<$ (i) $<$
6 (a) 130 (b) 0.3 (c) 24 (d) 12.12
7 (a) 2.7 (b) 10.075 (c) 12.47
8 (a) 7 (pieces) r 1.1(metres) (b) 23
(bottles) r 0.25 (litres) (c) 8 (hours)

1.10 Division of fractions (1)

1 A **2** C **3** $\frac{1}{a}$, $\frac{q}{p}$ **4** 4, $\frac{1}{10}$
5 12, $\frac{3}{4}$ **6** 1 **7** $\frac{2}{15}$ **8** 6
9 (b) $\frac{5}{3}$, (c) $\frac{5}{8}$, (d) $\frac{3}{7}$, (e) $\frac{48}{125}$,
(f) $1\frac{11}{17}$ **10** $\frac{3}{16}$ **11** $\frac{1}{2}$

1.11 Division of fractions (2)

1 D **2** C **3** $\frac{4}{7}$ **4** $\frac{5}{2}$ **5** 40
6 $\frac{3}{5}$ **7** $\frac{49}{20}$ **8** 5 **9** (a) $\frac{20}{27}$,
(b) $\frac{5}{21}$, (c) $\frac{1}{8}$, (d) $\frac{5}{42}$ **10** $2\frac{7}{10}$ **11** $\frac{5}{2}$
12 $\frac{3}{2}$, $\frac{11}{4}$, $\frac{1}{3}$, 2, $\frac{5}{3}$, 3, 0

1.12 Converting between fractions and decimals

1 B **2** A **3** C **4** 125, $0.\dot{1}2\dot{5}$
5 456, $1.234\dot{5}\dot{6}$, 1.2346 **6** $\frac{7}{10}$, 0.7
7 $\frac{357}{250}$, 1.428 **8** (a) $0.\dot{2}$, (b) $1.\dot{2}\dot{7}$
(c) $2.1\dot{3}$, (d) $3.8\dot{3}$ **9** 75.95 cm
10 (a) $0.\dot{3}$, (b) $0.2\dot{7}$, (c) $0.041\dot{6}$,
(d) $0.4\dot{6}$ **11** (a) $\frac{2}{5} < 0.\dot{4}\dot{0} < 0.\dot{6}\dot{2} < \frac{5}{8}$,
(b) $4.\dot{9}0\dot{5} < 4\frac{19}{20} < 4.\dot{9}\dot{5} < 4.9\dot{5} < 4\frac{24}{25}$

12 $0.\dot{1}$ $0.\dot{2}$ $0.\dot{3}$ $0.\dot{4}$ $0.\dot{5}$ $0.\dot{6}$ $0.\dot{7}$
$1.\dot{5}$ $1.\dot{8}$ $2.\dot{7}$ $3.\dot{3}$ $5.\dot{7}$ $8.\dot{1}$

1.13 Calculating interest and percentage

1 D, C, B, A **2** D **3** C **4** 15 750
5 9.01% **6** 3 013 043.48 **7** 92 000
8 2 **9** £20 360 **10** (a) £351
(b) Lee's suggestion will yield more interest.
£528 more.

Unit test 1

1 B **2** D **3** C **4** C **5** D **6** C
7 A **8** (a) 30 (b) 0.48 (c) 0.04
(d) 0.07 **9** $\frac{4}{33}$, $\frac{5}{9}$ **10** $\frac{32}{99}$ **11** 103
12 6 **13** $\frac{5}{12}$ **14** $0.7\dot{7}\dot{2}$ **15** 1.44%
16 30 **17** 40 **18** 3 **19** (a) 100
(b) 1780 (c) 17.6 (d) 31 000 **20** (a) 18,
54 (b) 7, 105, (c) 6, 168 (d) 2, 180
21 (a) 10.25 (b) 0.1 (c) 11.16 (d) 7.2
22 (a) $\frac{15}{2}$ (b) $\frac{42}{11}$ (c) $1\frac{3}{20}$ (d) 18 (e) 54
(f) 2.08 **23** 181 bottles can be filled up, and
0.45 litres will be left over (Hint: 100÷0.55 =
181 r 0.45) **24** 25.4 (times) **25** 22 cm
(Hint: a and b could be 28 cm and 1 cm, or
14 cm and 2 cm, or 7 cm and 4 cm; only 14 and
2 have lowest common multiple 14. So the
perimeter is $2 \times (14+2) = 32$ cm.)
26 £107 600 **27** He will pay £13.50 for the
interest tax. He will receive £5256.50.

Chapter 2 Rational numbers

2.1 The meaning of rational numbers

1 C **2** C **3** A **4** $+90°$ **5** 0
-1 **6** $-3, -2, -1$ **7** Answer may
vary, for example, 5.5 and 6.2. **8** 54.2
9 Make a loss of £78, The temperature
dropped by 8°C, The cost of a product
increased by 20% **10** Integers: 12, -1, 0;
Non-negative rational numbers: 12, 0.25, 0,
$\frac{1}{4}$, 80%; Fractions: 0.25, $\frac{1}{4}$, 80%, -0.4

⑪ $-2, -1, 0, 1, 2, 3$ ⑫ 22.7 m [Hint: $22 + (1.5 - 1 - 0.8 + 2.2 + 1.8 + 1.2) \div 7 = 22.7$ m] ⑬ (a) Answer may vary, for example, Part A: $1, 2, 3$; Part B: $-1, -2, -3$; Part C: $0, 5, 10$ (b) A: Non-negative integers B: integers C: non-negative numbers.

2.2 Number lines

① D ② B ③ D ④ origin, positive direction, unit length ⑤ 0 ⑥ $b - a$

⑦ -5 ⑧ 5 ⑨ right, $\frac{7}{4}$ ⑩ A: $1\frac{1}{3}$, B: $-\frac{2}{3}$, C: $-1\frac{1}{3}$ ⑪ A: 1, B: $-2\frac{1}{4}$, C: $-1\frac{2}{3}$, D: $\frac{3}{4}$ Points clearly shown on the number line as described. ⑫ $x = \frac{2}{5}$

⑬ 1 or 4 (Hint: Point B represents 2. When point C is on segment AB, point C represents 1. When point C is on the extension of segment AB beyond B, point C represents 4) ⑭ $x < -\frac{1}{2}$

2.3 Addition of rational numbers (1)

① D ② D ③ D ④ $+, -,$
(i) $+, 0.5$; (ii) $-, -0.5$; (iii) $+, 1$; (iv) $-, -1$ ⑤ $-8, -2$ ⑥ $-\frac{23}{6}$ ⑦ $\frac{5}{6}$

⑧ $-\frac{5}{6}$ ⑨ (a) $-$, (b) $-$, (c) $-$, (d) $+$ ⑩ 13.4 ⑪ -3 ⑫ (a) It was 1 km away at east direction of place A. (b) 5th (c) 8.2 litres ⑬ -0.4 (a) 1.8 (Hint: $-1.2 + 0.2 \times 15 = 1.8$) (b) 4.8 (Hint: The sum of the first 13 numbers is zero, therefore, just calculate $1.4 + 1.6 + 1.8 = 4.8$ for the sum of the first 16 numbers)

2.4 Addition of rational numbers (2)

① C ② C ③ A ④ 0 ⑤ $-5\frac{1}{5}$

⑥ -8.8 ⑦ $-100\frac{1}{2}$ ⑧ $-\frac{1}{3}$

⑨ $-\frac{1}{2}$ ⑩ -18.5 ⑪ -2 ⑫ $-1\frac{5}{6}$

⑬ (a) Answer may vary, for example, $(-1) + 2 + 3 + 4 + (-5) + (-6) + 7 + (-8) + (-9) + (-10) + 11 + 12 = 0$. (b) $4, 1 + 2 + 3 + 4 + 5 + (-6) + 7 + 8 + 9 + (-10) + (-11) + (-12) = 0$

2.5 Subtraction of rational numbers

① C ② B ③ C ④ (a) 20 (b) 5 (c) 1.8 (d) -132 (e) 0 (f) 12 ⑤ -1

⑥ 16.5 ⑦ $\frac{13}{20}$ ⑧ $2\frac{3}{5}$ ⑨ $-\frac{3}{8}$

⑩ -4 ⑪ 16 ⑫ -5 ⑬ -3.9

2.6 Multiplication of rational numbers (1)

① D ② B ③ C ④ 1 ⑤ -117

⑥ $\frac{2}{9}$ ⑦ 1 ⑧ 0 ⑨ (a) $-$ (b) $+$ (c) $+$ (d) $+$ ⑩ -12 ⑪ -5

⑫ $-\frac{15}{2}$ ⑬ The greatest product: $\left(-\frac{5}{8}\right) \times (-24) \times 4 = 60$; The least product: $0.2 \times (-24) \times 4 = -19.2$

2.7 Multiplication of rational numbers (2)

① A ② A ③ D ④ 25 ⑤ -27
⑥ 15 ⑦ (a) $>$ (b) $<$ (c) $=$
⑧ (a) commutative law of multiplication. (b) distributive law of multiplication over addition ⑨ -12 ⑩ 0 ⑪ 96

⑫ -1245 ⑬ -1 ⑭ $\frac{1000}{1001}$ (Hint: $1000 \times \left(1 - \frac{1}{2}\right) \times \left(1 - \frac{1}{3}\right) \times \cdots \times \left(1 - \frac{1}{1001}\right) = 1000 \times \frac{1}{2} \times \frac{2}{3} \times \frac{3}{4} \times \cdots \times \frac{999}{1000} \times \frac{1000}{1001} = \frac{1000}{1001}$)

2.8 Division of rational numbers

① D ② A ③ A ④ $-25, -\frac{4}{9}$

⑤ $-\frac{2}{9}$ ⑥ $-\frac{70}{9}$ ⑦ $\frac{1}{3}$ ⑧ -6

⑨ $-\frac{5}{4}$ ⑩ $4\frac{1}{2}, 3, -1\frac{7}{20}, 0, 3\frac{3}{4}$

⑪ -8 ⑫ -5 ⑬ $-\frac{32}{63}$ ⑭ $\frac{1}{15}$

(Hint: The reciprocal of the original expression:

$\left(\dfrac{1}{2}-\dfrac{4}{5}+\dfrac{7}{8}-\dfrac{19}{20}\right)\div\left(-\dfrac{1}{40}\right)=\left(\dfrac{1}{2}-\dfrac{4}{5}+\dfrac{7}{8}-\dfrac{19}{20}\right)\times(-40)=-20+32-35+38=15,$

therefore, the original expression is $\dfrac{1}{15}$)

2.9 Powers of rational numbers

1 D **2** C **3** D **4** B **5** $\dfrac{1}{3}\times\dfrac{1}{3}\times\dfrac{1}{3}\times\dfrac{1}{3}$, one third to the power 4, one third to the exponent 4 **6** $\pm8,4$ **7** $a,4$

8 $(-2)^{100}$ **9** $-\dfrac{1}{8}$ **10** $-\dfrac{1}{9}$ **11** $-\dfrac{2^3}{3}<-\dfrac{2^2}{3}<-\left(-\dfrac{2}{3}\right)^2<-\left(-\dfrac{2}{3}\right)^3$ **12** $\dfrac{9}{4}$

13 0 **14** $0; x=-1; x^{2015}=-1$

2.10 Mixed operations of rational numbers (1)

1 B **2** C **3** A **4** 1 **5** 37

6 -17 **7** $-\dfrac{27}{2}$ **8** -13 **9** (a) No. The correct working of calculation is: The original expression $= 6\div\left(\dfrac{2}{6}-\dfrac{3}{6}\right)=-6\times6=-36$ (b) No. The correct working of calculation is: The original expression $=-9\times\dfrac{9}{5}\times\dfrac{9}{5}=-\dfrac{729}{25}$ **10** -2 **11** 57 **12** -8

13 -36 **14** -4

2.11 Mixed operations of rational numbers (2)

1 D **2** C **3** D **4** 24 **5** -2

6 even number, 0 **7** 1 **8** 0 **9** $\dfrac{16}{3}$

10 -3 **11** -70 **12** -6 **13** $-1\dfrac{1}{6}$

14 (a) $-\dfrac{62}{15}$, (b) $-\dfrac{23}{27}$

2.12 Expressing numbers in standard form

1 B **2** D **3** C **4** 4.56×10^7

5 1.205×10^6 **6** $-32\,000\,000$ **7** 11

8 1.6×10^8 **9** 3.75×10^3 m/min or 3.75 km/min **10** 4.266×10^7m **11** $0.07\times10^8<$

$7.91\times10^6<8.3\times10^6<1.2\times10^7<2.3\times10^7$

12 (a) 2, 3, 5, 5 (b) $m, n, m+n, m+n$

(c) The original expression $=(1.25\times8)\times(10^{11}\times10^{10})=10\times10^{21}=1\times10^{22}$

Unit test 2

1 D **2** B **3** B **4** B **5** A **6** D

7 3 **8** $-6\dfrac{3}{5}$ or $1\dfrac{2}{5}$ **9** -3.25×10^7

10 $>$ **11** $\left(-\dfrac{2}{3}\right)$ **12** $\dfrac{90}{49}$ **13** $\dfrac{3}{2}$

14 -162 **15** -24 **16** second **17** -7

18 -3 **19** 8 or 2 **20** 3.5 **21** -1

22 $\dfrac{1}{2}$ **23** -12 **24** $-\dfrac{11}{16}$ **25** (a) 3

(b) $+9-(-8)=17$(g) **26** $-\dfrac{1}{40}$ or $\dfrac{43}{20}$

Chapter 3 Linear equations

3.1 Establishing simple equations

1 B **2** D **3** equal **4** $-1, 2$

5 Coefficient: 2, 25, $-\dfrac{4}{7}$, 1; Degree: 1, 3, 3, 5 **6** (a) $x=\dfrac{4}{5}x+\dfrac{5}{16}$ (b) $\dfrac{4}{5}x-x=\dfrac{5}{16}$ **7** (a) $2x+3=11$ (b) $12-x^2=8$

(c) $x=4+\dfrac{1}{x}$ **8** (a) Let the radius of the circle be r cm, then $2r=64$ (b) Let the width be x cm, then $2(x+3x)=48$ **9** Let the number of dormitories be x, then $4(x-5)=3x+100$. There were 460 students.

3.2 Solutions to equations

1 C **2** D **3** solution **4** is **5** is not **6** is **7** is **8** -2 **9** $\dfrac{1}{2}$, is not **10** yes: ①③; no: ②④ **11** (a) Answer may vary, for example, $2x+1=0$ (b) Answer may vary, for example, $x-1=0$ (c) Answer may vary, for example, $3x-6=0$ **12** $\dfrac{3}{2}$

13 (a) yes, because $1^2-1=0$ and $(-1)^2-1=0$. (b) Answer may vary, for example,

$x^2 - 9 = 0$

3.3 Linear equations in one variable and their solution (1)

1 A **2** C **3** linear, one **4** linear, two **5** $x = 8$ **6** no **7** (a) $x = 22$ (b) $x = 2$ **8** (a) $x = 2$ (b) $y = -16\frac{1}{3}$ **9** $x = 3$ **10** $n = 0$ and $x = 3$ **11** $a = -1$

3.4 Linear equations in one variable and their solution (2)

1 B **2** B **3** $-3x + 6 = 12$ **4** $5x + 10 = -4x + 14$ **5** $x = \frac{17}{5}$ **6** $x = 4$ **7** $x = 6$ **8** $x = -7$ **9** $x = -10$ **10** $x = -1$ **11** $x = 7$ **12** $x = -\frac{23}{5}$

3.5 Linear equations in one variable and their solution (3)

1 C **2** D **3** D **4** $2(7x - 5) = 3$; $14x - 10 = 3$; -10 $14x = 10 + 3$; $14x = 13$; 14 $x = \frac{13}{14}$; $x = \frac{13}{14}$ **5** $x = -9$ **6** $x = \frac{15}{2}$ **7** $x = 7$ **8** $x = \frac{1}{2}$ **9** $x = \frac{1}{3}$ **10** $x = -1$ **11** $x = 9$ **12** $x = 7$

3.6 Application of linear equations in one variable (1)

1 A **2** B **3** $2a + ax\%$ **4** 16 **5** Year 7: 40 students, Year 8: 50 students, Year 9: 30 students **6** $\frac{173}{60}$ hours, 37 km **7** 22 km/h **8** £2400

3.7 Application of linear equations in one variable (2)

1 C **2** B **3** 180 **4** 28 **5** $\frac{25}{3}$ **6** length = 25 m, width = 11 m **7** £125 **8** $\frac{10}{3}$ days **9** 10 days **10** £1200

Unit test 3

1 A **2** C **3** A **4** A **5** $x = -3$

6 $x = \frac{4}{3}$ **7** $-\frac{3}{2}$ **8** 3900 **9** 1 **10** $x^2 - \frac{2}{5}x = -\frac{1}{2}$ **11** $x = 3$ **12** $x = \frac{40}{9}$ **13** $x = \frac{3}{5}$ **14** $x = 3$ **15** 71.5 m and 20.5 m **16** 37.5 **17** 10 rooms and 59 trainees **18** 11 km

Chapter 4 Line segments, angles and circles

4.1 Line segments and their lengths

1 C **2** D **3** D **4** D **5** two one **6** shortest **7** the line segment **8** 3; AB, AC, BC; BC; AB; A line segment is the shortest among the lines in the distance between two points **9** 2, 0 **10** 3 **11** diagrams drawn as described **12** diagram drawn as described **13** 1, 3, 6, 10 (a) 66 (b) $\frac{(n+1)(n+2)}{2}$

4.2 Constructing line segments, their sums and differences

1 A **2** D **3** B **4** D **5** segment, the sum, the difference **6** BD, AB, BC, AB **7** 5 **8** BM, AB, AM, BM **9** 18 **10** 4, 4 **11** 2.1 or 5.25 **12** $\frac{1}{2}$ **13** 3 **14** 7 or 3 **15** $AB = 7.5$ cm (Hint: Let the length of AB be $5x$ cm, then $BM = 3x$ cm) **16** $AE = 7.5$ cm, $DE = 5$ cm **17** diagrams drawn as described **18** diagrams drawn as described **19** diagrams drawn as described $BP = 3$ cm

4.3 Angle concepts and representations

1 B **2** B **3** A **4** D **5** one two vertex **6** three capital letters   a Greek letter in lower case   a number (answer may vary) **7** rotation **8** OB, OA, O **9** outside, inside, on **10** (1) $\angle BAC$ (2) α (3) x **11** 90, 180, 120 **12** $\angle MON$

or ∠*MOL*, ∠*KOL* or ∠*LON*, ∠*KOM*, 5, ∠*MON*, ∠*MOL*, ∠*NOL*, ∠*KOL*, ∠*KOM*
⑬ 45° east of south(or simply southeast) 15° west of south 60° west of north ⑭ diagram shaded as described ⑮ (a) ∠*BCE*, ∠*BCF*, ∠*BCD*, ∠*ECF*, ∠*ECD*, ∠*FCD* (b) ∠*ABC*, ∠*BAD*, ∠*ABF* (c) ∠*AFB*, ∠*BFC*, ∠*BFD*
⑯ 26

4.4 Comparing angles and constructing angles (1)

① C ② A ③ C ④ protractor, *E*, *B*, coincide with, same side, inside ∠*ABC*, coincident with, outside ∠*ABC* ⑤ equal to, greater than, smaller than ⑥ coincident, coincident ⑦ interior ⑧ diagram drawn as described ⑨ diagram drawn as described ⑩ diagrams drawn as described ⑪ 10 angles, 15 angles, 21 angles, $\frac{1}{2}(n+2)(n+1)$ angles

4.5 Comparing angles and constructing angles (2)

① A ② D ③ B ④ A ⑤ (1) diagram drawn as described (3) *O*, *a* (4) *C*, *EF*
⑥ *C*, *O*, *D* ⑦ 3 ⑧ (a) 4 angles of 30°, or 6 angles of 60° (b) 2 angles of 120° (c) 4
⑨ ∠*A* = ∠*B* = 160° ⑩ (a) (b)

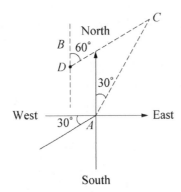

⑪ 4°

4.6 Constructing sums, differences and multiples of angles (1)

① B ② B ③ C ④ B ⑤ ∠*BOD*, ∠*BOD*, ∠*AOB*, ∠*BOC*, ∠*AOD* ⑥ 68°
⑦ 38°, 52° ⑧ 20, 50 ⑨ 3
⑩ ∠*ABD*, ∠*DBE*, ∠*BDC*, ∠*EDC*
⑪ 48°, 94°, 80° ⑫ 40°, 65° ⑬ α = 61°, β = 29° ⑭ angles drawn as described
⑮ ∠*EOC* = β − 90° ⑯ 150° or 10°
⑰ 138°

4.7 Constructing sums, differences and multiples of angles (2)

① B ② D ③ B ④ 137° ⑤ 3
⑥ 64° ⑦ $\frac{1}{4}$ ⑧ 30, 15, 5 ⑨ 64°, 32°
⑩ 11 ⑪ 20 ⑫ 175°, 46°, 70°, 69°
⑬ 19°, 31° ⑭ 54° ⑮ 118° ⑯ (a) 50°
(b) 15°

4.8 Complementary angles and supplementary angles

① B ② C ③ A ④ C ⑤ 45, 90
⑥ 90 ⑦ 60, 120 ⑧ 45 ⑨ γ, β
⑩ 51°, 141°, 90° ⑪ 40°, equal
⑫ 110° ⑬ 82° ⑭ 600, 50 ⑮ 18°
⑯ 25° ⑰ complementary angles: ∠*QOH*, ∠*NOH*. supplementary angle: ∠*PON*
⑱ 3422

4.9 Circle and its circumference

① D ② C ③ C ④ A ⑤ 2π*r*, 4π
⑥ 62.8 ⑦ 2.57 ⑧ 5 ⑨ 18.84
⑩ 10 31.4 9 56.52 11 22 ⑪ 2 m
⑫ 58.24 cm ⑬ 11.304 m ⑭ 20 minutes

4.10 The area of a circle (1)

① B ② C ③ B ④ π*r*² 3.14
⑤ 12.56 ⑥ 14 ⑦ 12.56 ⑧ $\frac{1}{4}$
⑨ 21.98 ⑩ 41.12 cm, 100.48 cm²
⑪ 251.2 cm ⑫ 18.84 cm, 113.04 cm²
⑬ The area of the question mark is largest, so more paint is used on it. (Hint: $S_{\text{Full stop}} =$

$\pi(R^2 - r^2) = 3\pi r^2$, $S_{\text{Comma}} = \frac{1}{2}\pi R^2 = 2\pi r^2$,

$S_{\text{Question mark}} = \pi R^2 - \left(\frac{1}{4}\pi R^2 - \frac{1}{4}\pi r^2\right) = \frac{13}{4}\pi r^2$)

⑭ 1334.5 cm² (Hint: The radius of the bigger circle is 4 times the radius of the smaller circle.)

4.11 The area of a circle (2)

❶ B **❷** A **❸** D **❹** 6 mm 18.84 mm

28.26 mm² 2.5 cm 5 cm 19.625 cm²

100 cm 628 cm 31 400 cm² 8 m 16 m

50.24 m **❺** $\frac{4}{9}$ **❻** 3 9 **❼** 1 1.57

❽ 21.195 cm² **❾** 50.24 **❿** 690.8 m²

⑪ The area of peonies is 28.26 m² and the area of jasmines is 19.74 m². **⑫** 21.5 (Hint: The area of smaller square $= 14^2 - 4 \times \left(\frac{1}{2} \times 6 \times 8\right) = 100$. The side length of the smaller square is 10, which is the diameter of the largest circle.) **⑬** 30.84 cm (Hint: S_{Circle} : $S_{\text{Semi-circle}} = 1 : 2$, so S_{Circle} : $S_{\text{Bigger circle}} = 1 : 4$, $r : R = 1 : 2$. The circumference of the circle is 18.84 cm, $r = 3$ cm, so $R = 6$ cm. Again C_{Circle} : $C_{\text{Bigger circle}} = r : R = 1 : 2$, therefore $C_{\text{Bigger circle}} = 12\pi$ cm. So $C_{\text{Semi-circle}} = 2R + \frac{1}{2}C_{\text{Bigger circle}} = 30.84$ cm)

Unit test 4

❶ C **❷** B **❸** C **❹** B **❺** A **❻** D

❼ D **❽** line segment **❾** $\pi r + 2r$ **❿** 3

⑪ < **⑫** 4 **⑬** 67.5 **⑭** 101, 79

⑮ 118° **⑯** 15.7 **⑰** 65 **⑱** 54 **⑲** 30°

⑳ 45° **㉑** 85 **㉒** 5 cm or 13 cm

㉓ 15°, 105°, 150° **㉔** 113.04 **㉕** $\frac{1}{2}$ $\frac{1}{4}$

㉖ line segment drawn as described **㉗** angle drawn as described **㉘** 50° **㉙** diagrams drawn as described **㉚** 1.8 cm **㉛** The minute hand turned 60° and the hour hand turned 5° **㉜** 26.84 cm **㉝** 891 cm²

1100 cm² **㉞** 140° **㉟** 3.5, $\frac{4}{7}$ **㊱** 9.12 cm²

Chapter 5 Transformation of figures

5.1 Translation

❶ C **❷** C **❸** same same size

❹ 5, 90° **❺** 3 cm, MP **❻** 5 cm, AA'

❼ 3 **❽** diagram drawn as described

❾ diagram drawn as described **❿** diagram drawn as described

5.2 Rotation

❶ D **❷** B **❸** C **❹** D **❺** point A, point E, 30° **❻** A, $\angle CAE$, AE, 100

❼ A, 90°, 270° **❽** An equilateral

❾ 80°, $B'O$, 80 **❿** diagram drawn as described, 90° **⑪** diagram drawn as described

⑫ diagram drawn as described **⑬** (a) point A (b) 90° (c) A right-angled isosceles triangle (d) $\frac{17}{32}$ (Hint: for areas $S_{\triangle AEF} = S_{AFCE} - S_{\triangle EFC} = S_{ABCD} - S_{\triangle EFC}$)

5.3 Rotational symmetry

❶ D **❷** B **❸** $0° < \alpha < 360°$

❹ definitely, not definitely **❺** 3 **❻** 2, 120 **❼** 90, clockwise or anticlockwise 180, clockwise or anticlockwise **❽** 60°, 60°, 60°, 120°, 120°, 120°, 60°, 60°; figures of point symmetry: (1)(2)(3)(7)(8) **❾** diagram drawn as described; point symmetry figures **❿** (a) yes, yes, midpoint of AC (b) 3, point A, point C, midpoint of AC

5.4 Folding and figures with reflection symmetry

❶ C **❷** D **❸** B **❹** reflection symmetry, the line of symmetry **❺** equal, equal **❻** parallelogram **❼** 3 **❽** lines of symmetry drawn as described

❾

(answer may vary)

5.5　Reflection symmetry

1 D　**2** D　**3** perpendicular, bisected, perpendicular, bisected　**4** the symmetry line　**5** 75°, 15　**6** points drawn as described　**7** line segments drawn as described　**8** diagram drawn as described　**9** diagram drawn as described　**10** (a) (b) diagrams drawn as described　(c) midpoints, midpoints, perpendicular to, bisecting

Unit test 5

1 C　**2** A　**3** C　**4** C　**5** shape, size　**6** 90　**7** 180　**8** is　**9** 4, 72, rotational　**10** perpendicular, bisects　**11** $\angle CAE$　**12** 90, anti-clockwise　**13** equal (or perpendicular and equal to each other)　**14** diagram drawn as described　**15** diagram drawn as described　**16** diagrams drawn as described　**17** (a) diagram drawn as described　(b) diagram drawn as described　(c) 50 cm²　(d) No. No. By reflection symmetry　**18** (a) diagram drawn as described　(b) It is the point symmetry about point D　**19** Line segment BG coincides with line segment EC after it is rotated 90 degrees clockwise at point A. They may not always exist. When points B, A and G lie on a same line, they do not exist.　**20** (a) 60°, counter clockwise　(b) $\triangle BCD$ and $\triangle ACE$, $\triangle BCG$ and $\triangle ACF$, $\triangle DGC$ and $\triangle EFC$　(c) 80°

Chapter 6　Learning more about cubes and cuboids

6.1　The surface area of a cube

1 A　**2** C　**3** C, D, E　**4** $12a$, $6a^2$, 24, 24　**5** (a) 73.5 cm²　(b) 384 cm²　**6** (a) 54　(b) 36　(c) 8　(d) 27　**7** 864　**8** 15 000 cm²　**9** 120 m²　**10** 1140 cm　**11** 6.75 kg

6.2　The surface area of a cuboid

1 B　**2** B, C　**3** 13, 3, 4, 78, 104, 24,

206　**4** (a) 119.5 cm²　(b) 178 m²　**5** 27.06 m²　**6** 160 cm²　**7** 10 400 cm²　**8** 46 cm², 54 cm²　**9** 179 600 cm²

6.3　Change of surface areas (1)

1 B　**2** B　**3** B　**4** 4, 6, 8, 10; 18 cm², 24 cm², 30 cm², 36 cm²; 14 cm², 18 cm², 22 cm², 26 cm²　**5** (a) 24 cm²　(b) 32 cm²　**6** 11 250 cm²　**7** 36 cm²　**8** 34 cm², 24 cm²　**9** (a) 384 cm²　(b) 386 cm²　(c) 388 cm²

6.4　Change of surface areas (2)

1 C　**2** A　**3** 136, 112　**4** 4　**5** 4, 3, 2, 24　**6** 27, 972 cm²　**7** 96　**8** 72 cm²　**9** 41 200 cm², 480 000 cm³　**10** 384 cm²　**11** 1350 m²　15 000 tiles　**12** 128 000 cm³　**13** 304 cm², 286 cm², 256 cm², 248 cm², 236 cm², 268 cm²

6.5　Different parts of a cuboid

1 B　**2** C　**3** B　**4** 8, 12, 6　**5** edge AB, edge DC, edge HG, plane $BFGC$　**6** 48, 12, 5　**7** not necessarily, definitely　**8** 110　**9** 22.5 cm²　**10** 72 cm　**11** The object has 8 faces. The surface area: 350 cm²　**12** 115 cm³　**13** 648 cm³

6.6　Properties of cuboids: relationship between edges

1 B　**2** C　**3** B　**4** intersecting　**5** parallel　**6** edge AB, edge EF, edge HG; edge BC, edge CG, edge DA, edge DH; edge AE, edge EH, edge BF, edge FG　**7** 0, 6, 6　**8** 90 cm³　**9** (a) line AE　(b) line AD, line BC　(c) line AE, line BE, line DF, line CF　(d) line AD, line DF　(e) line AE, line DF　**10** (a) skew lines　(b) intersecting　(c) parallel　(d) skew lines　**11** 24 cm³　**12** There are 4 answers: 15 edges, 14 edges, 13 edges, and 12 edges.

6.7　Properties of cuboids: relationship between edges and faces

1 C　**2** C　**3** perpendicular　**4** edge

AB, edge EF, edge CD and edge HG

5 $ABFE$ and $DCGH$ **6** 12 cm **7** 32 cm³
or 64 cm³ or 128 cm³ **8** 48 **9** 20
10 126 cm², 90 cm³

6.8 Properties of cuboids: relationship between faces

1 D **2** B **3** C **4** C **5** A

6 $\alpha \perp \beta$ **7** $\alpha /\!/ \beta$ **8** plane $ABFE$, plane
$BCGF$, plane $CGHD$, plane $ADHE$ **9** plane
$ABCD$, plane $EFGH$, plane $ABFE$, plane
$CGHD$ **10** Height: $(36 - 8 \times 2) \div 2 =$
10(cm), the volume: 480 cm³ **11** (a) 40
(b) 10 (c) 2 or 5 **12** 18 000 cm³

Unit test 6

1 A **2** A **3** D **4** A **5** D

6 3, 1 **7** 1, 0 **8** 4 **9** 4 **10** 3 3
11 edge AB, edge CD, edge EF; plane $DCGH$
12 edge HG, edge CD, edge EF; edge AB,
edge BF, edge CD, edge CG; edge AD, edge
HE, edge CD, edge HG **13** plane $DCGH$,
plane $ABCD$ **14** 4 **15** 4 **16** 12 **17** 48
18 8 **19** 94 **20** Yes. Planes A, B, D, F
are perpendicular to plane C. **21** 180 cm²
22 40 cm² or 44 cm² or 46 cm² **23** (a) 3 cm
(b) 90 cm² **24** Length: 6 cm, width: 6 cm,
height: 1 cm, volume: 36 cm³

Chapter 7 Algebraic expressions: concepts, addition and subtraction

7.1 Using letters to represent numbers

1 A **2** C **3** D **4** $70\% m$

5 $a(b+c) = ab + ac$ **6** $\dfrac{a}{b} = \dfrac{am}{bm}$ $(m \neq 0)$

7 $100c + 10b + a$ **8** $\dfrac{1}{2}l - a$ **9** $(100 -$

$8a - 3b)$ (pounds) **10** $\dfrac{12a + 18b}{30} =$

$\dfrac{2a + 3b}{5}$ (score) **11** $\left(\dfrac{1000}{a} + \dfrac{1000}{b}\right)$(hours)

12 (a) 11 (matchsticks) (b) $(2n + 1)$
(matchsticks)

7.2 Introduction to algebraic expressions

1 B **2** D **3** D **4** $m-2n$ **5** $2(m-$
$n)$ **6** $a-b^2$ **7** $(a-b)^2$ **8** $\dfrac{1}{3}x+4$

9 $\dfrac{1}{3}(x+4)$ **10** $\dfrac{1}{3}(x-4)$ **11** $(1000 +$

$290x)$ (pounds) **12** $\dfrac{400}{x+y}$ (seconds)

13 $0.8 \times (1 + 40\%)a = 1.12a$ (pounds)

14 $\dfrac{80a}{a+10}\%$

7.3 Values of algebraic expressions (1)

1 D **2** B **3** B **4** 3 **5** $7\dfrac{1}{2}$

6 $-5\dfrac{5}{6}$ **7** 121 **8** $\dfrac{1}{60}$ **9** -23

10 $-\dfrac{5}{8}$ **11** -1 (Hint: from $a^2 - a =$

2015, we can get $a^2 - a - 2016 = 2015 - 2016 =$
$-1.$) **12** -6; $-\dfrac{2}{3}a - 2$ **13** 86℉, $\dfrac{5}{9}(x-$

$32)$℃ **14** (a) $\dfrac{4}{9}$, $\dfrac{1}{16}$; The pattern: $a^2 - 2ab +$
$b^2 = (a-b)^2$ (b) $(101.23 - 1.23)^2 = 100^2 =$
$10\,000$

7.4 Values of algebraic expressions (2)

1 D **2** B **3** D **4** $0.08m$, $0.92m$

5 $\dfrac{a}{4}$, $\dfrac{a^2}{16}$ **6** -7 **7** -1 **8** 35

9 21 **10** 0, 5 **11** 6 **12** $3\dfrac{3}{4}$

13 $\dfrac{mb}{a(a-b)}$(days), 10(days) **14** (a) $x \leqslant$
12, $2x$ (pounds), $12 < x \leqslant 18$, $(2.5x - 6)$
(pounds), $x > 18$, $(3x - 15)$ (pounds)
(b) £20, £34, £69

7.5 More about algebraic expressions

1 D **2** C **3** B **4** C **5** C

6 $0.8x^3 - 2x^2 + x - 5$ **7** $-3, 3$ **8** $\pi, 2$

9 3, $-\dfrac{1}{3}x^2y^2$, 4 **10** 4, $-3x^2y^3$ and $4x^5$, 5

11 2 **12** $n = 1$ and $m \neq 3$ **13** $m = 2$
14 $a = -2$ **15** Answer may vary, for
example: $3 - x + 2y - 4xy^2$, $5 + x^2 + 3y - 9y^3$
and so on.

7.6 Simplifying algebraic expressions: collecting like terms (1)

① D ② C ③ B ④ 7, 3 ⑤ $3x^2y$ and $6yx^2$, -3 and 7 ⑥ 3 ⑦ $-2x$

⑧ $\frac{10}{3}x^2 - \frac{8}{3}x$ ⑨ $0.4x^2y + 4.5xy^2 - 1$

⑩ $-6x^{n+1}y^2 - 4x^ny^n$ ⑪ $a = -2$, $b = 3$

⑫ $x^2 - 2y$, -3 ⑬ (a) $100x + 10x^2 + (2x - 1) = 10x^2 + 102x - 1$ ($x = 1$, 2, or 3)

(b) 111 243 395

7.7 Simplifying algebraic expressions: collecting like terms (2)

① A ② C ③ B ④ 4 ⑤ -1

⑥ 0.008 ⑦ 11 000 ⑧ $2x^2 + 2x + 1$

⑨ $16x^3 - 9x^2 - 5$ ⑩ $6x^2 - 2xy + 8y^2$, 53

⑪ -2140 ⑫ $\left(\frac{8}{3}x + 14\right)$ (students)

⑬ all are $\left(1 - \frac{\pi}{4}\right)r^2$

7.8 Adding and subtracting algebraic expressions (1)

① D ② B ③ C ④ $x + 2y - 3a + 4b$

⑤ $-x - 2y - 3a + 4b$ ⑥ $-2y - 4b$ ⑦ $2y - 3a$ ⑧ $-2x - 21y + 25z$ ⑨ $-3y^2 + 3y$

⑩ $-y^3 - 1$ ⑪ -1 ⑫ $\frac{13}{12}a^2b^3$, $-\frac{13}{3}$

⑬ $-3a^3 + a^2 + 12a - 14$, $-8\frac{1}{8}$ ⑭ Let the

five consecutive positive integers be n, $n + 1$, $n + 2$, $n + 3$, $n + 4$, and the sum of these numbers is $5n + 10$, which is divisible by 5.

7.9 Adding and subtracting algebraic expressions (2)

① B ② C ③ D ④ $b - c - d$ ⑤ $b^2 - b$ ⑥ $-2x^3 - 5x^2$ ⑦ $2x^3 + 5x^2$ ⑧ $2x^3$

⑨ $-5a + 5b$ ⑩ $\frac{5}{6}x^2 - 4xy + \frac{14}{3}$ ⑪ $x^3 - 3x^2 + 4$ ⑫ $-x^2 + \frac{5}{3}xy - \frac{1}{4}y^2$ ⑬ $-a^2b - 4ab^2$, -3 ⑭ Let the order of thousands place, hundreds place, tens place and ones place of the four-digit number be a, b, a, b,

then this four-digit number is $1000a + 100b + 10a + b = 101(10a + b)$, which is divisible by 101.

7.10 Adding and subtracting algebraic expressions (3)

① D ② C ③ A ④ $\frac{4}{3}a + b$ ⑤ $\frac{5}{3}x + \frac{8}{5}y$ ⑥ $-1.9x - 1.4y$ ⑦ $2.1x - 0.6y$

⑧ $x + 3y$ ⑨ $\frac{5}{2}x + \frac{11}{2}y$ ⑩ 2 ⑪ 50

⑫ $(130 + 2x)$ degrees ⑬ Let the digit in the tens place of the two-digit number be a, and the digit in the ones place be b, then the three-digit number with x in the left side of y is $M = 100a + 10b + y$, and the other three-digit number with y in the left side of x is $N = 100y + 10a + b$. The difference of the two numbers is $M - N = 90a + 9b - 99y$, which is a multiple of 9. ⑭ Answers may vary, for example: $5x^2 + 6x + 7$, $-2x^2 - 5x - 8$ and so on.

Unit test 7

① D ② B ③ C ④ D ⑤ B ⑥ B

⑦ $6a^2 - 3$ ⑧ $a(b - c) = ab - ac$

⑨ $3a^2 - 4b^3$ ⑩ $-x^3y - \frac{2}{3}x^2y^2 + 4x + 5y^3 - 7$ ⑪ 3 ⑫ $-a + b + 3x$ ⑬ $-5m + 6n - 3y$ ⑭ (a) $(x + 20) \times \frac{3}{4} - 10$ (b) 5 $\frac{35}{4}$

⑮ $a^2 - 5ab$ ⑯ $4a^2 + 1.5ab + 2b^2$ $518\frac{1}{4}$

⑰ $x^3 - 7x^2 + 22x - 12$ ⑱ $-x + y^2$; $\frac{5}{2}$

⑲ Yes, let the digit in the tens place be a, and that in the ones place be b, then any two-digit number can be written as $10a + b$. After swapping the digits in the number, the new two-digit number is $10b + a$. The sum of these two numbers is $(10a + b) + (10b + a) = 11a + 11b$ or $11(a + b)$, which is a multiple of 11.

⑳ $5000 + 300x$ (pounds) £6125 ㉑ Answer may vary, for example: $x^3 - x^2 + x - 1$ and $3x^3 - 5x^2 + x + 1$

Chapter 8 Multiplying algebraic expressions

8.1 Multiplying powers with the same base (1)

1 B **2** D **3** D **4** $(-2)^{18}$

5 $(-a)^{21}$ **6** a^{3m-n} **7** $\left(-\dfrac{1}{8}\right)^7$ **8** $(a+b)^9$ **9** $7a^2+30a^5$ **10** $18a^4-5a$ **11** a^9-3a^7 **12** $-(a-b)^5$ **13** 100 **14** a^3b^2

8.2 Multiplying powers with the same base (2)

1 B **2** B **3** C **4** 2^{2013} **5** 0

6 $162x^5$ **7** $2(a-b)^7$ **8** 3 **9** 18

10 $\dfrac{27}{2}$ **11** x^3y **12** $(x-y)^{n+3}$

13 (a) 10^9 (b) 10^{2n+3} **14** $a+b=c$

8.3 Multiplying algebraic expressions (1)

1 B **2** C **3** A **4** $3a^3b^4$

5 $-15a^5b^5$ **6** $25a^5{}^nb^{4n+2}$ **7** 2×10^7

8 2.31×10^9 **9** $-(x-y)^{m+10}$

10 $-3x^2y^{n+1}$ **11** $-\dfrac{25}{2}x^{20}y^{20}$ **12** $-\dfrac{31}{16}x^{11}y^{10}$

13 $m=4$, $n=\dfrac{12}{5}$ **14** -261

8.4 Multiplying algebraic expressions (2)

1 B **2** A **3** D **4** $-2xy+2x^2$

5 $-5x^3y^2z+3x^2y^3z$ **6** $-x^4y^2-\dfrac{4}{3}x^3y^3+\dfrac{8}{15}x^2y^4$ **7** $x^{n+1}y^{n+2}-x^{n+1}y^n+x^{n+2}y^{n+1}$

8 $2(x+y)^{10}-3(x+y)^{n+2}(x-y)^n$

9 $6xy^3$, $-10xy$ **10** 33 **11** $-6a^3b+3a^2b^2$, 9 **12** $x=\dfrac{1}{4}$ **13** $x=\dfrac{1}{3}$ **14** -7

(Hint first to get: $-m+n=5$ and $mn=-6$, then the original expression $=2mn+(-m+n)=-12+5=-7$)

8.5 Multiplying algebraic expressions (3)

1 B **2** D **3** A **4** $a+b$ **5** ac, $ad+bc$ **6** $ab-4a+3b-12$ **7** $6x^2+5xy-6y^2$

8 $9a^2-4b^2$ **9** $8a^3-b^3$ **10** -4

11 (a) $x^3+6x^2+11x+6$ (b) $-4x^3-12x^2+x+3$ (c) $x^2+y^2+2xy-4x-4y+4$

12 (a) $a^{2n}-2a^nb^n+b^{2n}$ (2) $a^{3n}+b^{3n}$

13 $x=-6$ **14** The area increased: $(4a+4)\,\text{cm}^2$, the volume increased: $6a^2+12a+8\ \text{cm}^3$

8.6 Multiplying algebraic expressions (4)

1 D **2** B **3** A **4** $3x^7y^8$

5 $\dfrac{1}{9}x^4y^2-x^3y^3$ **6** x^2-4y^4 **7** $8ab$

8 a^4-b^4 **9** $1+a^6$ **10** $x+5$

11 (a) $a^2-4b^2+12b-9$ (b) $a^3+9a^2+26a+24$ **12** $x=-1$ **13** $a=1$, $b=0$

14 (a) $a=-2$, $b=3$ (b) $12x^2+x-6$ [Hint: $(3x-a)(4x+b)=12x^2+17x+6$, and $(3x+a)(x+b)=3x^2+7x-6$, so $-4a+3b=17$, $a+3b=7$, $-ab=6$]

Unit test 8

1 D **2** D **3** D **4** B **5** B

6 $(-3)^{33}$ **7** a^{1111} **8** 30 $10\,000$

9 3 2016 **10** $13\,000$ **11** $-24x^5y^3$

12 $a+b$ ab **13** $2a^2+5ab+2b^2$ **14** $-5x^2+6xy-y^2$ **15** $9n^2-2m^2+3mn$ **16** $72p^2q^3$

17 96 **18** $10y^2+4xy$ 114 **19** (a) $4x+520$ (b) £9720 **20** $3\ \text{cm}$

Chapter 9 Events and possibilities

9.1 Introduction to possibility

1 C **2** D **3** definitely, impossible, possibly **4** (a) A (b) A (c) B

5 (a) △ (b) √ (c) × (d) △ (e) √ (f) × (g) √ (h) △ (i) × (j) ×

6 (a) Colour all the 4 cubes blue. (b) None of the 4 cubes is coloured blue. (3) Colour 1 or 2 or 3 cubes blue **7** (a) C (b) C (c) A or B (d) B or C

9.2 Comparing possibilities: how likely is it?

1 (a) B (b) D **2** C **3** more

4 less **5** a notebook   a pencil case

6 Colour 3 sections red, 1 section yellow.

7 Colour 3 sections red, 1 section green, 2 sections yellow and 2 sections blue. **8** No, it's not a fair game. Method 1: Change the game rule to "If the ball Joan picked is greater than 3, then she wins. If it is smaller than 3, then Matt wins." Method 2: Change the condition "There are 6 identical balls in a bag and each ball is marked with 1, 2, 3, 4, 5 and 6 respectively." ⑨ (a) Kath has the same possibility as Lin has. (b) Kath has greater possibility (c) Kath has less possibility ⑩ (a) A three-digit number (b) a multiple of 3

9.3 Working out possibilities (1)

① D ② D ③ A ④ 3 12, 16, 20 ⑤ (a) 4 (b) 6 (c) 10 ⑥ (a) $3 \times 4 = 12$ (b) 5 (c) 4 (d) 4 (e) 11 ⑦ (a) 4 Tom, Mary, Joseph, Ian (b) 12 Tom, Mary; Tom, Joseph; Tom, Ian; Mary, Tom; Mary, Joseph; Mary, Ian; Joseph, Tom; Joseph, Mary; Joseph, Ian; Ian, Tom; Ian, Mary; Ian, Joseph ⑧ (a) 24 (b) 4 (c) 0 (d) 15 (e) 6660 [Hint: $(1+2+3+4) \times 6 \times 111 = 6660$]

9.4 Working out possibilities (2)

① B ② B ③ (a) 18 (b) 6 (c) 10 ④ 432 (selections) ⑤ (a) 36 (b) 18 (c) 20 ⑥ (a) 120 (ways) (b) 48 (ways) (c) 36 (ways) ⑦ 576 (ways)

9.5 Events of equal possibility

① D ② C ③ C ④ $\frac{1}{3}$ ⑤ $\frac{2}{5}$ ⑥ $\frac{1}{3}$ ⑦ $\frac{1}{4}$ ⑧ $\frac{1}{2}$ ⑨ $\frac{1}{2}$ ⑩ (a) $\frac{1}{6}$ (b) $\frac{1}{3}$ (c) $\frac{1}{2}$ ⑪ $\frac{1}{6}$ ⑫ (a) $\frac{1}{2}$ (b) $\frac{2}{9}$ (c) $\frac{1}{6}$

Unit test 9

① green, white ② (a) possibly (b) definitely (c) impossible (d) possible (e) impossible ③ (a) A (b) C (c) B

(d) C ④ neither of them ⑤ more ⑥ 24 ⑦ 28 ⑧ $\frac{1}{6}$ ⑨ B ⑩ B ⑪ A ⑫ C ⑬ B ⑭ (E)——(1) (D), (E)——(2) (B)——(3) (C)——(4) (D)——(5) ⑮ (a) No, it is unfair, because the possibility is not equal. (b) Answer may vary, for example: Dawn wins if the card she draws is greater than 5. Lucy wins if the card is smaller than 5. ⑯ (a) Red (b) Blue (c) $\frac{3}{8}$ ⑰ (a) White (b) 3 ways (Add 2 yellow balls; Take away 2 white balls; Add 1 yellow ball and take away 1 white ball) ⑱ 20 They have the same possibility ⑲ (a) Odd number (b) 9 (c) Even number (d) $\frac{9}{25}$ ⑳ (a) $\frac{2}{7}$ (b) $\frac{1}{3}$

End of year test

① C ② A ③ D ④ C ⑤ D ⑥ B C ⑦ D ⑧ C ⑨ D ⑩ C ⑪ B ⑫ B ⑬ B ⑭ D ⑮ C ⑯ 260 ⑰ 6.28 ⑱ 6.5348×10^7 ⑲ 3 or 27 ⑳ 40° west of south ㉑ 2 ㉒ 6 ㉓ FG ㉔ $-x^4$ ㉕ $x^2 + x - 6$ ㉖ 6 ㉗ possibly ㉘ 10 ㉙ 74° ㉚ $4n$ ㉛ 0.5 ㉜ 120, 12 ㉝ $4x^2 + 8x - 15$ ㉞ $x = -53$ ㉟ (a) 10, 12, 13, 20, 21, 23, 30, 31, 32 (b) an even number (c) $\frac{1}{3}$ ㊱ (a) Diagram drawn as described. (b) 10 ㊲ (a) £22 (b) £1035.20 ㊳ 12 km/h ㊴ (a) Triangle $A_1B_1C_1$ drawn as described. (b) Triangle $A_2B_2C_2$ drawn as described. (c) Answer may vary. ㊵ (a) 50.24 m² (b) 25.12 tons

Notes

Notes

Notes

Notes

Notes

Notes

Notes

Notes

Notes